Samuel Thompson Lowrie

The Lord's Supper

According to the directory for Worship of the Presbyterian Church in the

United States of America

Samuel Thompson Lowrie

The Lord's Supper
According to the directory for Worship of the Presbyterian Church in the United States of America

ISBN/EAN: 9783337283803

Printed in Europe, USA, Canada, Australia, Japan

Cover: Foto ©Lupo / pixelio.de

More available books at **www.hansebooks.com**

ACCORDING TO THE DIRECTORY FOR WORSHIP

OF THE

Presbyterian Church in the United States of America

MAINTAINED AS THE TRUE SCRIPTURAL FORM FOR ITS OBSERVANCE,
BOTH AGAINST PRESENT ATTEMPTS TO CHANGE IT, AND ALSO
AGAINST MODIFICATIONS IN USE BY OTHERS

BY

SAMUEL T. LOWRIE

Chaplain of the Presbyterian Hospital, Philadelphia

Second Thousand

ENLARGED BY AN ARGUMENT MAINTAINING THE WINE PROPER FOR THE COMMUNION

CONTRIBUTED BY THE

REV. DUNLOP MOORE, D.D.

New Brighton, Pa.

1888

THE LORD'S SUPPER

CONTROVERSIAL tract on the Lord's Supper may be a most edifying and comforting composition. It is not essential to controversy that it should be, as it often is, distracting to *all* who are engaged in it. It is sometimes most potent to draw some men together, and unite them more firmly than ever in the communion of what is imperilled. The matter of controversy, if it be worth controversy, becomes more precious in view of the danger that threatens it.

The most effective controversial effort is that which so represents the value of the thing contended for as to make it appear worth maintaining even through conflict. Then the relish of the truth involved is keener than in a situation where that truth is enjoyed in perfect peace. In the present immunity of the churches from persecution, there is not that intense enjoyment of the ordinances that was felt by those who were compelled to seek them by stealth, meeting in glens and caves. There seems to be even an apathy attending that central and most significant ordinance of all, the Lord's Supper, because the freedom to observe it in the right way has long been unassailed. By reason of that apathy, it is now in danger of mutilation and diversion from its proper use and profit. Through very frivolity of secure possession, what was once stoutly and often fiercely maintained, at the risk and even cost of life, is now easily surrendered and trifled away by neglect. One great contention of the Reformation of the sixteenth century concerned the right of the laity to the cup in the Lord's Supper. It was the right to partake of the cup of wine—*i.e.*, of the wine itself—which Christ appointed for all his disciples, saying, "*Drink ye all of it.*" It was the right to partake of the wine of which he said, "*This is the new covenant in my blood for the remission of sins.*" But now that the churches have so long enjoyed this right without dispute, many are ready to surrender what was secured through such bloody conflict. We say, surrender the cup that the Reformers gave us. For, however innovators may view the cup that contains their substitution for wine, it is certain that the Reformers never endured their mighty conflict concerning the cup, that they might fill it with whatever they thought best. And it is certain that, had they regarded the wine of the cup an indifferent matter, they would never have made the right of the laity to use the cup a matter of contention.

We now find ourselves, however, in a situation that makes controversy necessary, if we would preserve to the churches the cup that the Reformation gave back into the hands of the laity. God has allowed this to come about, perhaps, in order to arouse the churches from their indifferent appreciation of this most precious ordinance, the Lord's Supper; an indifference that naturally attends the unmolested enjoyment of it, as it does most good things that are enjoyed in the same way. Our attention is drawn to one particular of defection, in the matter of the wine, just referred to. But that is only the place of the breaking forth of the evil. A proper estimate of the situation revealed by that is, that the mischief extends to the whole subject of the Lord's Supper. A proper effort to stay the mischief, then, will not be to confine oneself to arresting the innovations concerning the cup; we must review the whole ordinance in the light of the particular mischief assailing one part.

A spirit of supposed liberality prevails in religious life, and radically affects the posture of professing Christians toward every religious subject. Once the first question was, What is the truth we must confess and practice and maintain? Now the interest in every truth that has been maintained is chiefly the question, What has been held too strictly? What may be yielded? In this interest every subject in religion is reviewed, and every question that has been closed is reopened. The Apostolic injunction is: "*Whereunto we have already attained, by that same rule let us walk.*" This is a rule indispensable to progress, and was once much heeded. But now the things that have been "attained"—*i. e.*, ascertained—and have long been the rule by which Christians have safely walked, are assailed from within the Christian ranks; and the right to assail them has been easily and generally allowed, till there is practically, if even unconsciously, widespread doubt whether the Church has really attained to anything—*i. e.*, ascertained anything—that should be a rule for all to walk by and think alike about. It is obvious that there never was anything in religious practice about which the catholic Church so absolutely thought the same thing and walked by the same rule, as that it is wine that must be used in the proper observance of the Lord's Supper. We cannot expect to see the Church attain to greater unanimity in any other matter than was attained in that. If, then, this matter was and is not a clear case for the application of the Apostolic injunction cited above, we must conclude that the Apostle has proposed an impracticable rule.

The spirit that is abroad has assailed the doctrine and

practice of the Presbyterian Church in regard to the Lord's Supper, as we see; and we will confine our attention to that. But we must measure the full extent of the effect. It is, as we have said, a mistake to suppose that the mischief is confined to the one matter of the wine. It could not have affected the readiness to change that we see in that particular without affecting the sentiments regarding other particulars of the Lord's Supper, and, in fact, the whole ordinance. Some external occasion has only to arise, and we may see the effort made to modify the ordinance in some other particular to suit the occasion. It is idle to say there is no danger of that, because we cannot see how it can arise. Only a century ago, and no one could have suspected that there would spring up a movement to change the wine of the ordinance. It is now even easy to conceive the possibility of a movement to change from the use of common bread to unleavened bread, or of a movement to change from common bread of grain-growing countries to the staple diet of countries that do not raise grain.

So much more is said about liberality in religion, and against strict observance of ordinances as they have been received and long used, that what has been well said in favor of such scrupulous observance has been forgotten by many; and what is still well said is drowned in the noise of the voluble innovators. Thus, by many even who would walk in "the old paths," it is unsuspected how much is to be said in favor of what they would wish to do, and would have all do.

The effort of this tract will be to show that there is ever so much to be truthfully said in defense and favor of a scrupulous adherence to the observance of the Lord's Supper in that form that has been prescribed in the Standards of the Presbyterian Church in the United States of America.

Though we shall study conciseness in expression, we will allow also that fullness of representation that the subject itself demands. We shall not, indeed, attempt to go over all the ground, for that is impossible, even if one were to write only on what is proper to the subject itself, apart from the controversies connected with it. As well might one attempt to go over the whole plain that lies between the Missouri River and the Rocky Mountains. Yet one may, like a traveller, go over some of that wide plain, and end the exploration on an eminence that permits him to see it stretching to the horizon, with no visible boundary, and suggesting the idea of its being limitless.

The briefest, yet sufficient statement of our doctrine of the Lord's Supper is given in the answer to Question 96 of the Shorter Catechism: "The Lord's Supper is a sacrament, wherein, by giving and receiving bread and wine, according to Christ's appointment, his death is showed forth; and the worthy receivers are, not after a corporal and carnal manner, but by faith, made partakers of his body and blood, with all his benefits, to their spiritual nourishment and growth in grace."

The precise directions for the observance of the Lord's Supper are found in the Directory for Worship, chap. ix. § 5: "The table, on which the elements are placed, being decently covered, the bread in convenient dishes, and the wine in cups, and the communicants orderly and gravely sitting around the table (or in their seats before it), in the presence of the minister, let him set the elements apart, by prayer and thanksgiving.

"The bread and wine being thus set apart by prayer and thanksgiving, the minister is to take the bread, and break it, in the view of the people, saying, in expressions of this sort:

"'Our Lord Jesus Christ, on the same night in which he was betrayed, having taken bread, and blessed and broken it, gave it to his disciples; as I, ministering in his name, give this bread unto you; saying [here the bread is distributed], Take, eat; this is my body, which is broken for you; this do in remembrance of me.'

"After having given the bread, he shall take the cup, and say:

"'After the same manner our Saviour also took the cup; and having given thanks, as hath been done in his name, he gave it to the disciples; saying [while the minister is repeating these words, let him give the cup], This cup is the new testament in my blood, which is shed for many, for the remission of sins; drink ye all of it.'

"The minister himself is to communicate, at such time as may appear to him most convenient."

This doctrine of the Lord's Supper and of the mode of its observance the Presbyterian Church maintains as Scriptural and proper, in the sense that this and no other is the true doctrine, and that this mode and no other is the proper mode of observing it. To this position our church came through much conflict. Every particular was something "attained" at the cost of bitter controversy and much suffering. The table for the elements, and not an altar; common bread, and not a wafer; the wine as the privilege of the laity, and not for the priest alone; the minister ministering in the name of Christ, and communing with the rest, and not a priest offering a sacrifice; the communicants seated as at a table, and not bowed on their knees as adoring a mystery; these and still other particulars were established by appeal to Scripture, and through bloody conflicts and cruel martyrdom.

If what was so won were only not wrong, or only right

as some other modes of observance might also be right, there would seem to be reason enough for scrupulously observing what our fathers gave us as so precious in their sight and attained at such cost. This could only bring us a blessing such as the Rechabites had from God for keeping inviolate the rule of living that their father gave them. It would be attended in us with a zeal for a true and Scriptural worship of God like that of the Reformers, which would bless the world as their zeal has done. It is absolutely essential as the true embodiment of a spirit of reverence for them and their work, and as the token that we believe they contended righteously. Departure from what they won and handed down reflects on the wisdom of what they did, and condemns the zeal that animated them. Departure from a single particular involves this condemnation, for they contended to blood and martyrdom for every one of these particulars.

But while these present proper motives for scrupulous observance of the above directions for observing the Lord's Supper, they are secondary and much inferior to the primary motives. These primary motives are the same that animated the Presbyterian Reformers themselves in adopting and maintaining them. The primary motive of all must be the belief that what is so prescribed is essential to the proper observance of the Lord's Supper; that in this manner and no other is the Lord's Supper properly observed. Such is the meaning of our church as expressed in its Standards.

By this it is not meant, that we do not recognize other modes of observing the Lord's Supper, that other Christians use, as being the Lord's Supper; or that such observance must be without the blessings that attend that ordinance. We distinctly recognize the contrary of this with reference to many whose practice differs from our own. We believe the ordinance may be faultily observed and yet be owned by Christ. We do not pretend that all of our own worship is faultless; yet we expect a blessing. But we hold to our way of observing the Lord's Supper as the right way, carefully derived from Scripture. We hold that the ordinance is of such importance that it is a solemn duty to observe it scrupulously in what we believe to be the right way. We hold that what is to be done is by express command from our Lord, and that nothing so commanded, or understood to be so commanded, can be treated as indifferent. We hold, then, that we are not permitted to conform to the ways of others who differ from us, for the sake of outward unity in the sense of outward likeness.

Yet it is to be understood that this position is maintained in reference to what we observe for ourselves, and regarding rules made for us all who are of the same church. This is not a bar to our individually joining with our fellow-Christians of other churches in observing the Lord's Supper in their way, where they encourage such fellowship. Jeremiah, after years of protest and struggle to keep the Jews from seeking shelter in Egypt, and denouncing the ruin that God would send on such a course, followed his erring people thither, when nothing would restrain them; and he voluntarily suffered with them. And we who are aware of the faulty worship of others, may have sufficient motives for joining with them at times; motives arising out of our identity with them. But this need never be, and ought never to be, at the cost of suppressing our own convictions, or of surrendering our right and duty to proclaim them, or of ceasing to try and persuade our fellow-Christians to adopt these convictions.

In the present matter of contention about the wine of the Lord's Supper, we censure no one who, having the same convictions as ourselves, still joins his fellow-Christians of any

Presbyterian Church in observing the Lord's Supper, though they have rejected the use of wine. On the other hand, however, we honor such as refuse to do this while there are Presbyterian Churches left that remain faithful to the Confession and Directory for Worship. To such we say, Let us join hands, and, like Jeremiah, let us do all we can to persuade our fellow-members of the Presbyterian Church to abide in this our Jerusalem; let us dissuade as many as we can from departing to that Egypt of illusive hope under banners of temperance fanaticism. Those who have gone there, and those who will go there, will fare no better than did the Jews under Pharaoh-hophra. If, indeed, the whole communion of Presbyterians go there, as the leaders of this movement boastfully claim will come about, it will be time enough then for us to decide whether, Jeremiah-like, we will follow and share the disastrous consequences. But, for our part, we apprehend no such result. Our confidence, however, can only be sustained by a Jeremiah-like constancy in adherence to the "old paths," and in warning against the danger of leaving them.

Up to the present writing, our General Assembly has, in its deliverances, adhered with constancy to our Standards. It is supposed, indeed, by many, that the action of the General Assembly of 1881 sanctions what we now remonstrate against. This, however, is not true. The deliverance is as follows: "The essential elements of the Lord's Supper are bread and wine. The General Assembly has always recognized the right of each church session to determine what is bread and what is wine. In the judgment of the Assembly no new legislation is needed on this subject." It is obvious that by this it can no more be intended that a church session may determine that what is not wine is wine, than it can be intended that for bread a session may give communicants a stone. The right of church sessions recognized in this action is expressly measured by what the Assembly "has always recognized"—*i. e.*, by precedent. One of these precedents is the action of 1877: "The control of this matter is left to the sessions of the several churches, with the earnest recommendation that the purest wine obtainable be used." And this action was reiterated in 1885. There never was a recognition by the General Assembly of a right to use at the Lord's Supper anything but bread and wine.

We are confronted along the whole line of particulars mentioned above as essential to the proper observance of the Lord's Supper with variations in the mode of observing it. Leaving out of view the Romish Mass, there are the denominations that we recognize as evangelical. The Lutherans insist on unleavened bread; the Episcopalians receive the elements kneeling; many in both these communions hold more and some entirely to the notion of an altar instead of a table; the Irvingites observe the Supper in a fashion to represent it as distinctively eucharistic worship; and now among Methodists and Congregationalists, and, alas! Presbyterians, many reject wine and substitute something else, and this practice appears to some extent also in the Protestant Episcopal Church.

This makes it necessary to consider the question:

WHAT IS ESSENTIAL TO THE PROPER OBSERVANCE OF THE LORD'S SUPPER?

The first step to agreement about this must be a clear understanding as to *what is the test or criterion of what is essential.*

It is evident that many suppose that the test of this matter is discovered by the question: Do these variations in observing the sacrament make it untrue in the sense of unreal? do they serve as an obstacle to the blessings that the sacrament signifies and seals? Reflection, however, shows that this affords us no clue. For, supposing that the blessings intended by the Lord's Supper do attend the faulty observance of it, they are not of a sort that admit of observation and of inference from them. The blessings that extend to all time, until Christ shall come again, cannot be estimated till that time has ended. The blessings that concern the individual who partakes of the Lord's Supper (and it is these that are meant) are known only to himself, and afford no ground for others to reason from. And, even the person himself, does he properly infer that he has observed an ordinance without fault or error because he has a blessing? Perhaps many persons do so; but it is an ignorant mistake when it is done. God's providence in general, and his gracious dealings in particular, encourage us to expect his blessing when we sincerely seek it, in spite of our faulty use of the means he has appointed us to use to obtain it. The water flowed from the rock when Moses sought water for the people by smiting the rock. Nevertheless Moses sinned in smiting the rock. It was essential to the proper observance of that Old Testament sacrament (1 Cor. 10 : 4), observed only once, that Moses should speak to the rock. Neither he nor the people were permitted to infer that the speaking was unessential, and that smiting did as well, because the intended blessing came all the same. Moses suffered for the change he effected in the observance; and with him Aaron; and also all the people suffered by the displeasure God visited on Moses and Aaron. And this bids us reflect that the blessing did not come all the same, spite of the smiting. The water came forth; but how much more blessing might have attended the gift of the water had Moses not sinned there, but did not attend it, no man can measure. And what is missed by the faulty observance of the Lord's Supper no man can measure, or even suspect. This must not be ignored because a blessing has been received.

The case of Moses affords the proper and exact illustration of how we must find the true and only test or criterion of what is essential to the proper observance of the Lord's Supper. It is the same for every divine ordinance. The simple inquiry is, What is commanded? All that is commanded, in every particular of the command, is essential. Moses was not only to procure the water from the rock; he was to do it in the manner commanded. The Lord's Supper is to be observed because Christ commanded it. It is to be observed with a view to procuring the blessings attached to it. But it is to be observed in the manner he commanded, if it is to be his Supper, and if it is to be attended by the blessings proper to it. He said, "*Do this.*" Whatever, then, he commanded to be done is essential to the proper observance of the Lord's Supper.

Where do we find Christ's commandment directing how his Supper is to be observed?

Here it has become important to affirm, that no distinction may be made or attempted between what Christ commanded and what the Apostles delivered to the churches. This is assumed in the Standards of our church, which appeal to all parts of the New Testament as of equal authority, and as being the word of Christ. There is especial illustration of this in our Directory for Worship, chap. ix. § 4, when it says: "The minister shall show, That this is an ordinance of Christ; by reading the words of institution, either from one of the evangelists, or from 1 Cor. xi. chap."

The distinction objected to, however, has become common of late. Introduced by rationalizing tendencies, it has crept into the purest churches. Many, accordingly, appeal to the evangelists (Matthew, Mark, Luke) to ascertain what Christ commanded about the Lord's Supper; not as to part of the testimony of the Apostles themselves, but as better than that; better than 1 Cor. 11: viz., as being as nearly as possible the testimony of Christ himself. Thus there is felt a satisfaction in the result obtained, though it may agree with 1 Cor. 11, as if it had been obtained in an original manner from the same source from which the Apostles derived what they delivered. The result is then relied on as if it were founded on the authority of Christ himself, and not of his Apostles. It is but a step from this position when one proceeds, as many nominal Christians do, to correct the deliverances of the Apostles by a supposed better comprehension than theirs of Christ's own testimony. This is to suppose that we may, in the matter of ordinances, attain a position toward the Apostles like that of the Samaritans to the woman who told them of Christ, when they said, "*Now we believe, not because of thy speaking; for we have heard for ourselves.*"

All this is illusory, as a matter of fact, owing to the very nature of the New Testament Scripture. But it is also a hurtful error. Christ never meant that his Church should so get past his Apostles to himself. He said, "*He that heareth you, heareth me.*" The Apostle Paul says, "*If any man thinketh himself to be a prophet, or spiritual, let him take knowledge of the things which I write unto you, that they are the commandment of the Lord.*" (1 Cor. 14:37.) And he says we are "*built upon the foundation of the apostles and prophets, Christ Jesus himself being the chief corner stone.*" (Eph. 2:20.) To which may be added, the words of the Apostle Peter: "*I write unto you, that ye should remember the commandment of the Lord and Saviour through your apostles.*" (2 Pet. 3:2.)

We are, then, an Apostolic Church, in order to be a Church of Christ. The Apostles gave the ordinances to the Church, and what they command is the commandment of Christ. When, therefore, we observe the ordinances of Baptism and the Lord's Supper, we do so, not primarily as *imitating* the example of the Apostles in obeying Christ's appointment so to do. We observe them because the Apostles delivered them to the Church, and as *obeying them* by whom Christ commands us. In regard to the Lord's Supper, therefore, we are to make no difference between the evangelists and 1 Cor. 11 as sources of information, except as the passages themselves assume to be authoritative for the matter under consideration. But our inquiry is, What did Christ command the *churches* to do in celebrating his Supper? On this point it is obvious that 1 Cor. 11 is more our guide than the narratives of the evangelists, for it is instruction precisely for the case; it is the Apostolic Directory for Worship in this matter. The evangelists, on the other hand, as narrating the sayings and doings of Christ, are less precise and explicit about what the Church shall do. They do not write primarily for that purpose; they give much matter beside. The Apostle delivers the ordinance for observing the Lord's Supper. The evangelists recount the history of the original institution of the Lord's Supper.

In the original observance of the Lord's Supper there were many circumstantials, some of which are evidently no part of the Lord's Supper; others are less evidently so. It is noticed that at the original Supper it was night; only men were present; they reclined at the table; unleavened bread was used; there was other food used beside bread and wine; there was a considerable interval between dispensing the bread and the cup. The question is raised: How shall we know what of these is essential to the Lord's Supper, and what not?

The reply is, We are not left to determine that. The Apostle determines all that for us by his directory, given in 1 Cor. 11. That is the Scriptural and only warrant both for what is essential to the observance of the Lord's Supper and for what may be omitted or changed in the circumstantials of its original observance. The omissions or changes are by Apostolic authority. They are not the result of private judgment in Christians. There may not be more or other omissions or changes made by the private judgment of Christians, as if profiting by the wisdom and practice of the Apostles, and improving on that, in the spirit of enlightened liberality. Even Paul makes no pretense of acting on his own judgment in the omissions and changes that he authorizes. He says, "*I received of the Lord that which I also delivered unto you.*"

We look, then, to 1 Cor. 11 as the precise directory for worship in this matter. Being such as it is, the Apostolic ordinance, we ought, therefore, so to accept it, as a matter of course. But if this be not assented to as a matter of course in the proper spirit of subjection to the Apostles, the correction of such waywardness comes by the logic of history. The controversies about the manner of observing the Lord's Supper show that a rule of practice, to which all must conform as authoritative, is needed, if we would see all Christians observe the Lord's Supper in the same way. And this is a matter wherein it is important that there should be precise uniformity. It is not only desirable, it is important, that, wherever the Lord's Supper is celebrated, it should be in a way to appear at once to be the same Supper that Christ appointed and that Christians everywhere observe. It, with Baptism, is the signal mark of having one Lord and one faith. We believe, therefore, that, with all Christians who do as we do, we are setting the example of observing the Lord's Supper in the only true way, by scrupulously following the directions the Apostle Paul gave to the Church in Corinth, as the only authoritative rule for all Christians.

HOW WAS THE LORD'S SUPPER COMMANDED TO BE OBSERVED?

From the Apostle's directions it appears, that *the Lord's Supper is to be observed by congregations of believers assembled for worship.*

This is essential to the institution. It is a communion, *i. e.*, a common participation of many—that is, of all that make the same company—in the same thing. From this the ordinance receives its appropriate name: The Communion. It is not to be observed alone, or in private. That would not be the Lord's Supper. Thus, when the Lord's Supper is desired by any one who, on account of sickness or anything else, is unable to appear in the regular assembly of the Church, it is necessary that the assembly should be represented in his sick-room, or wherever he may be, by a greater or less concourse of his fellow-Christians. Only by an actual communion with fellow-disciples can the observance be the Lord's Supper. Observing the rest of its forms without this communion deprives what is done of the proper character of the Lord's Supper. It is not what Christ commanded when he said, "*Do this.*" It is, therefore, not the Lord's Supper.

This, though not the contention of all the Reformers of the sixteenth century Reformation, was the contention of what is distinctively known as the Reformed Theology. It was eminently so of the Presbyterian Reformers of Geneva, France, and Scotland. They not only rejected the Romish Mass as observed in the churches, but private Masses and all private

Communion. The Directory for Worship prepared by the Westminster divines, and adopted by the Church of Scotland, while giving very full directions for religious visitation of the sick, makes no provision for the observance of the Lord's Supper in the sick-room for their benefit. The same is true of the Directory for Worship adopted by our own church. Practically the Lord's Supper is sometimes celebrated in sick-rooms in the manner already described; but naturally the occasions are rare. And where a Scriptural and true apprehension of the nature of the ordinance prevails, it will rarely be desired.

The Lord's Supper is to be observed by itself, without combination with a general meal of varied diet.

The situation of the church in Corinth, that had been reported to the Apostle Paul, led him to give precise directions to this effect. He shows that he thought that they ought so to have understood his original deliverance of the Lord's Supper to them. Many of them, however, had not so understood. They brought various and much provision to their assembly for an ample meal. As was natural to persons that could so act, they did not even share their abundance generously with those who could bring less or nothing. Some ate in a gluttonous way, and some drank wine to drunkenness, while others were left hungering. With such indecent feastings they combined eating bread and drinking the cup as observing the Lord's Supper. The Apostle sharply chides all this, and tells them to do their eating and drinking, where this is done for themselves, at their own houses. Of what they had been doing he says: "*When therefore ye assemble yourselves together, it is not possible for you to eat the Lord's Supper.*" Thus he denies even the name of the Lord's Supper to that manner of observing it that they had been using.

By this we are taught that the mere intention of eating the Lord's Supper does not make what we do the Lord's Supper. The manner of observing it is important to make what we do the Lord's Supper. What is essential to the Lord's Supper is not found only in the bread and wine, and using them as appointed, whether we use them with or without other things in combination. Mixing their use with other things is confounding the Lord's Supper with what is not that, and deprives what is done of the right to be called the Lord's Supper. The Lord's Supper must be observed by itself as something deserving to be done for itself alone. And such observance the Apostle enjoins.

This, as it concerns a promiscuous meal, is so universally recognized as the rule for the Lord's Supper, as to need no amplification. But though there is little example of combining the Lord's Supper with meals of abundant and varied diet, there is much example of combining what is precisely prescribed in the Apostle's directory with things not there prescribed. We believe that where that is done, we are warranted, by the Apostle's treatment of the doings in the church of Corinth, in affirming that "*it is not possible to eat the Lord's Supper.*"

The Lord's Supper is a meal, to be eaten together by those whose meal it is.

The Apostle calls it *kuriakon deipnon*, which is appropriately translated, *the Lord's Supper*. It is natural for the ordinary reader to suppose that the word *supper* designates an evening meal, as it does with us; and the inference is, that it is so named because Christ instituted the ordinance at a meal eaten at night. The name *deipnon*, however, has no such significance. It was the name the Greeks gave to the principal meal of every twenty-four hours, as we call the same meal *dinner*. The hour for eating it varied, as the hour for dinner, so called, with us, according to the fashions of the time and place. In Homer it was a midday meal, as dinner is with us in times or places of simpler manners. In Corinth, in Paul's day, it was eaten at evening time, as many with us dine at six o'clock. At least such was the usage of those whose manners are most reflected in the literature of the times. *Deipnon* was the name given to a picnic meal, where each brought his contribution to what was to be consumed. It was especially the name used for what was intended to be a feast.

It is not uncommon to hear Christians express themselves as if there were a special fitness in celebrating the Lord's Supper at night, and justifying the sentiment in the manner already referred to. We see, however, that not only is there no ground for this in the name, Supper, but that, rightly understood, the name the Apostle uses signifies something very different. It is express warrant for regarding the fact that it was night when Christ instituted this ordinance, as unessential to the ordinance itself. The name *deipnon* signifies that the meal is to be regarded as the important religious meal of Christians, and as such, a feast. But the time of taking it is to be determined by convenience, like the time of any other *deipnon*.

Being essentially a meal, *the Lord's Supper must be set forth as a meal.*

The elements to be consumed are therefore to be placed on a table, and those who assemble for the Lord's Supper are to assemble with the table so spread before them as for a meal. And when partaking of the elements, this must be done as partaking of a common meal. All this is obvious from the directions in 1 Cor. 11, and from the very name, Supper.

It is evident enough that the Romish Mass is a total

departure from what is thus prescribed. Instead of a table, there is an altar, as for a sacrifice. It is not a meal that is prepared, but a sacrifice is offered. The disciples do not dispose themselves to eat together, but prostrate themselves, as adoring a mystery of the actual body and blood of Christ.

There has been, and continues to be, much division of sentiment among Presbyterians in regard to the form of the table proper to use in the Lord's Supper. Many insist on the importance of its being a table of such extent that all the congregation may sit down to it together, or, if the congregation be too large for that, in large companies in succession. There is no doubt of the propriety and impressiveness of this custom, where it may be conveniently observed; but it is evident, by reference to the Apostle's directions, that it is not prescribed. Nothing more is prescribed than what is involved in the name *deipnon*. It is essential that the elements be set forth as for a meal, and that the participants be disposed so as to receive of the same meal all together. At any *deipnon*, or feast, where the company is too great to be gathered at one table, it is a simple device to distribute the food to them from a common table, which needs only to be large enough to set on it the food of the feast. This must often have occurred at what Corinthians called a *deipnon*. It is, therefore, strictly proper for the Lord's Supper to be set on a small table before the communicants, where these are in great number, as they are in every church. It is a marring of the observance, rather than a strict observance, where it is made necessary to surround a table in successive large companies, making a first and second and third table of what should be made one simultaneous meal.

The proper provision for the Lord's table is bread and wine.
By this is meant, that bread and wine are essential, with-

out which, to use the Apostle's expression, "*it is not possible to eat the Lord's Supper.*" By this is meant, also, that nothing besides bread and wine may be used. There has been and continues to be much contention about both the bread and the wine. There is, however, little room for contention where Christians, in due subjection to Apostolic authority, are agreed to observe scrupulously the directions of 1 Cor. 11.

In proper order, *the bread first claims our attention.*

The first contention has been whether leavened or unleavened bread must be used. The Church of Rome contends for unleavened bread, against the Greek Church which insists on only leavened bread. The controversy dates back to an early period of Christianity. Among Protestants, since the Reformation of the sixteenth century, the Lutherans have contended for unleavened bread against the Reformed churches who freely allow the use of either leavened or unleavened bread, while giving the preference to leavened bread as the more common sort of bread, and believing that it is the common bread of any community that is proper bread to be set on the Lord's table.

The necessity of using unleavened bread is maintained by appeal to the occasion of the original institution of the Supper, which was at the Jewish Passover, where unleavened bread was used. It was such bread that Jesus brake and gave to the disciples, and said, "*Do this in remembrance of me.*" If, then, we would scrupulously do what he commanded, taking his own action as indicating what we must do, we must use the same sort of bread that he used. That such is our duty, is supposed to be enforced by the consideration that the Lord's Supper is a perpetuation of the Jewish Passover in a Christian form, and that, having its root in that institution, it was the intention of our Lord to transfer from it to his own new institution the bread that was ordained for that Passover. As additional confirmation of its being his intention that unleavened bread must be used, appeal is made to the symbolic import of leaven, and of unleavened bread. For this it is supposed we have the express direction of the Apostle Paul himself, who gives us the directory of 1 Cor. 11, when in 1 Cor. 5:7, 8 he says: *"For our Passover also hath been sacrificed, even Christ: wherefore let us keep the feast, not with old leaven, neither with the leaven of malice and wickedness, but with the unleavened bread of sincerity and truth."*

Regarding the last-named consideration, Paul evidently represents a Passover-keeping that is Christian: but he represents the Passover as having been slain, which was Christ himself, a slaying that was over and past, and the feast as actually being kept. This, as written to distant readers, who would not receive the communication for many days, would have no fitness, if said of a solemnity like the Lord's Supper that these readers might be celebrating, even if it were Easter and protracted through a week. He evidently refers to the one slaying of Christ, as the antitype of the Passover lamb, and as being our Passover, and to the subsequent feast time as one that goes on lastingly; so that while the Christian lives he is keeping that feast; and the exhortation is, to keep that feast in the strict observance of a pure and guileless life, which is expressed symbolically by unleavened bread, which was used at the original Passover. And such *is* the old Passover in its Christian form. The Apostle draws the likeness, not from the yearly observance of that feast, but from the occasion of its first institution. In that transaction the Israelite saw himself and his people ransomed from an old life of bondage, to go forth to the promised land in the enjoyment of a free life of the service of God. All that after-life was the consequence of what then took place, and was to be a feast of life, which should be as free from corruption as the bread they ate at the starting was free from leaven. The Christian life has a similar beginning in the death of Christ, who is our ransom, and should be one continual feast of guileless living.

Such being the Apostle's meaning in the metaphor of 1 Cor. 5 : 7, 8, not only does it exclude any reference to the Lord's Supper; it also precludes our regarding the Lord's Supper as the annual Passover feast expressed in New Testament form.

There is, however, a relation between the annual feast of the Passover and the Lord's Supper. It is detected in the relation which each bears to the great original dispensation of God that it commemorates. The annual Passover feast commemorated the deliverance by which God drew out the children of Israel to be his people, with which was connected prophetically the redemption that was finally to appear for them, and to come to all the world through them. Our Lord, in accomplishing that redemption, institutes for his people a new commemoration, which is to show forth what he has done. He does this, appropriately and significantly, on the last occasion of his observing the old Passover, as recognizing the connection of the new with the old. But what he instituted he calls the new, and what he tells his disciples to do is *this* that he now does, as intimating that henceforth it is *this* ordinance that they are to observe, and not the one they had just been observing.

Thus the Lord's Supper is historically related to the feast of the Passover, and has its roots in it, as the new dispensation in Christ is related to the original Passover and the exodus from Egypt, and has its roots in that.

But such being the case, there is no ground for inferring that it was intended to transfer the elements of the Passover feast that Christ used for his Supper to his own ordinance, as a mark of that relation existing between them. The drift of inference is the other way. It is all in the direction of what is amplified in the Epistle to the Hebrews, where the former dispensation (and the annual feast of the Passover was part of it) is represented as growing old even in Jeremiah's time, with the destiny of wholly vanishing away. (Heb. 8 : 13.) It could not be the purpose of our Lord to perpetuate a vestige of it by incorporating it into his new institution.

As for the symbolical meaning of leavened and unleavened, there is no such unvaried use of these as to justify our assuming that symbolism is meant when it is not expressed; and when it is meant, all depends on what is expressed. Jesus compared the kingdom of heaven to leaven hid in a lump of meal. (Matt. 13 : 33.) There is no reference in any inspired account of the Lord's Supper to any symbolism of the unleavened quality of the bread that Jesus used.

The only thing left that bears on the question whether unleavened bread must be used at the Lord's Supper is the fact that Jesus used such bread when instituting the Supper. That fact would be decisive in such a matter, if we had only the accounts of the evangelists to direct us. But we have Apostolic direction how the Lord's Supper must be observed, and that is our primary authority. The situation in the church of Corinth revealed gross abuses. They were making a gluttonous feast of what ought to be the Lord's Supper. The Apostle writes to correct the abuses. There can be no question that the bread they brought to such feasting was common, leavened bread, and they had used this for the Lord's Supper. The Apostle proposes no correction of this use. He would only restrain them to the use of such loaves for the Lord's Supper along with wine, without bringing any other food. *The Apostle,* therefore, *shows that it is proper to use common, leavened bread at the Lord's Supper.*

This finds corroboration in Apostolic example. Immediately after the day of Pentecost, as we find it reported of the new disciples, "*They continued steadfastly in the Apostle's teaching and fellowship, and in breaking of bread and in prayers.*" And it is further reported: "*And day by day, continuing steadfastly with one accord in the temple, and breaking bread at home, they did take their food with gladness and singleness of heart.*" (Acts 2 : 42, 46.) "*The breaking of bread*" was observing the Lord's Supper, which they did in connection with a common meal of varied diet. But the feast of unleavened bread was over many days before. The day of Pentecost had come, at which feast two loaves of leavened bread were offered even in the temple itself, as an act of solemn worship. There was no rule prescribing unleavened bread in the homes of the Jews. They had returned again to leavened bread, as the common bread of daily use. In such a situation it would need to be precisely expressed that "the breaking of bread" was with unleavened bread, and not with the bread in common use, if such was the fact. There is, however, no such intimation. Therefore it is justly inferred that the earliest Apostolic example of observing the Lord's Supper was with common, or leavened, bread.

As has been mentioned in the foregoing, the Lord's Supper was observed in these earliest instances in connection with a common meal. We notice, then, that the directions in 1 Cor. 11 for its observance by itself was a correction of the earlier mode. The correction is founded in the reasonableness of the thing. The presumption is that this modification of the earlier practice had been established also by the other Apostles. The Apostles were sensible men, and what they ordained was agreable to good sense. It is not likely that what the Church has universally approved as decorous for the Lord's Supper was so late in suggesting itself to the Apostles generally that it was not till Paul regulated the practice in Corinth that the Lord's Supper was observed by itself. We believe that too much has been inferred in this way from the few notices we have of the *Agapæ*, or love feasts of the earliest Christians.

We ascertain by the foregoing, that the Apostolic directory, when prescribing bread as essential to the Lord's Supper, must be understood as sanctioning the use of common, leavened bread. This, however, is no disapproval of unleavened bread, which is also proper. It does, however, reprove those who would insist on unleavened bread as essential or even important to the Lord's Supper, and who would refuse the name of Lord's Supper to an observance that uses leavened bread.

But *there are other questions about the bread.* For, allowing that the bread may be unleavened or leavened, we know that common bread was made of the meal of oats, rye, barley, and spelt, as well as of wheat, and the finest of wheat, in Palestine and the countries where the Apostles planted churches. And we know that in other countries it is now made of maize or Indian corn, of rice, of chestnuts, of fish, etc., etc. In the Arctic regions and among uncivilized people of the tropics the diet of the people furnishes no name for what we mean by bread. The equivalent for that staple diet would be a word representing very different kind of food.

The practical question has been presented: *Is the material of the bread essential? or, May that be used which, in non-grain growing countries, takes the place that bread has with us?*

With regard to countries that grow the same grains as Palestine, the question presents no perplexity. It is certain, on the one hand, that in Palestine bread was commonly made of all the grains named above as growing there. The kind of bread used would be determined by the condition of the family, and by the agriculture of particular regions. The gospel rule was to eat such food in any house as that house would set forth. It is, therefore, a certain inference that the Apostles would use in "the church in the house," such bread as the occasion offered, both for their own refreshment and for observing the Lord's Supper. The same liberty, therefore, is proper in all similar situations. But we know, also, that the Jews, like people of all countries that raise the same grains, regarded that as the best bread that was made of "the finest of wheat." Though barley meal was used in worship (Num. 5:15), it was held to be a meaner offering, while the noble offering was of fine wheat flour. (Lev. 2:1.) Whatever was proper, and would still be proper, for the observance of the Lord's Supper in a special emergency, it is evident, that where the Lord's Supper was to be observed with studied propriety, the promptings of self-respect and decorum would prescribe that the best bread attainable should be used, viz., bread of fine wheat flour. And, as might be expected, the references of the earliest Christian archives, both inspired and uninspired, suggest to the reader only that such bread was used.

The same motives of self-respect and of decorum must be influential now in determining what is essential to the proper observance of the Lord's Supper. Our Directory for Worship says, "The table on which the elements are placed, being decently covered." The study of such decency is universally recognized as essential to acts of worship. This is sufficiently regulative, and will regulate the kind of bread to be used in grain growing countries for the Lord Supper as it has heretofore done.

But the question about the material of which the bread must be made is supposed to present a different aspect in countries that can raise no wheat, and can procure wheat flour only with great difficulty. The same question relates to wine, and seems more pressing in that case because of the greater difficulty of transport and of preservation. We will consider both bread and wine in this connection. To put it plainly: *May the Lord's Supper be observed in North Finland by using dulse for bread, and reindeer milk, or mead, or spirits for wine?*

This is a question of practical importance in heathen missions, and has been earnestly debated in the missionary fields. In China, the debate has been especially about the wine, because no wine is produced there. The practice has differed with different missionaries. Some have thought it proper to use some spirituous drink that is a native production; others may use some drink not wine, that has no alcoholic quality; others deem it important to use only wine, spite of the difficulty of obtaining it, and of the ignorance of it among the Chinese. The debate and the divergence of views on the present subject is no new thing. The affirmative of the above question may be found asserted by authorities in the Western or Roman Church previous to the Reformation of the sixteenth century. Among the Genevan theologians after the Reformation, the distinguished Bucan and, later, Pictet affirm the same thing. Among the latest continental Reformed theologians, Ebrard represents the same view. We are not acquainted with any discussion of the subject by theologians of the English tongue not in the missionary field.

The question now under review deserves an earnest consideration even as a case *in thesi*, for it is specially fitted to bring into clear light what one understands or believes about the Lord's Supper.

It is quite natural and logically necessary that the Romish notion of a sacrament should lead one to deem it necessary to observe it with any convenient substitute, when the proper element is not at hand. That doctrine represents the sacrament and saving grace as so connected that one is not to be had without the other. Thus Baptism may and ought to be administered by some one not ordained for the ministry, if such a minister cannot be got. There is not time to call the minister to one dying; let, then, the sister of mercy, or let the nurse or any Christian, baptize him; for baptism is necessary to regeneration. In the same way the sacrifice of the Mass is necessary to absolution from sins. If bread and wine cannot be had, let something else be used, that perishing souls may not be deprived of the grace the church procures by that sacrifice. Yet, though holding such views, it is likely that the Romish church, on missionary ground, makes fewer exceptions from the strict use of the proper wafer and the wine, than Protestant missionaries from proper bread and wine.

We think that it will appear, on examination, that the supposed necessity of observing the Lord's Supper without proper bread and wine, where these are not at hand, arises from mistaken sentiments about the ordinance, and especially from the mistaken notion, still clinging to Protestants as a remnant of the old Romish superstition, that there is grace, saving grace, connected with the Lord's Supper that is not to be enjoyed without it; and that as Christ would not deny one of his people any of the grace he gives, so that grace that only attends the Lord's Supper must be offered them by such means as are at hand, if the proper elements are not. There is not the same sentiment manifested about Baptism. However it may be with other denominations, Presbyterians have always been free from regarding it as having grace so connected with it, that in order that its grace may not be missed it must be administered, without regard to what is important to its most proper administration. We hold that it should be administered only by an ordained minister. It is to be deferred till it can be administered in that proper form. If a dying man desires it, or a parent for a dying child, it is still not to be administered without the proper minister. It is sometimes even deemed important to deny baptism in such cases, that the anxious soul may not be betrayed into trusting to the efficacy of a rite, for that grace which is received by faith in Christ alone. We have the same sentiment and pursue the same way with reference to the Lord's Supper in particular cases. We refuse to administer it to the dying; we do not allow it to be the Lord's Supper if one partakes of the bread and wine alone; the former, because we would not have a dying man rest his confidence on a rite, and because the Lord's Supper is appointed for living Christians to show forth the death of Christ; the latter, because the outward sign of the communion that is essential to the ordinance is wanting when one is alone.

But the plain instances just appealed to involve two very important doctrines concerning the Lord's Supper. The first is, that all the grace needed for salvation by a believer may be enjoyed without the use of the sacrament. The second is, that a sacrament is a rite that has its own proper form, without which it is not that rite. Therefore, when it must be observed with omission of something of that proper form, if observed at all, then it must be left unobserved.

But why make a distinction between one essential part of the rite and another? Why say, It is not the Lord's Supper if there be no company of believers to be the sign of communion; and not say, It is not the Lord's Supper if there be no bread and wine such as the Apostles appointed?

Especially is this a pertinent inquiry, in view of the fact that it is deemed essential to the ordinance that it should be administered by an ordained minister. All the historic churches agree in this. All are represented in those regions where it supposed that necessity justifies the use of substitutes for bread and wine. Why, then, teach believers there that there can be no Lord's Supper without the minister, and not teach also that there is no Lord's Supper without the appointed bread and wine? These elements are everywhere more easily obtained than the ministers. And we believe it is plainer that bread and wine are essential to the proper observance of the Lord's Supper than that the presence of the ordained minister is; though we fully believe the latter also.

In some of those same regions where it is thought necessary to use substitutes for bread and wine—*e. g.*, Finland and Iceland—there are found those who count it a privilege to provide their tables as tables are set in London, Paris, Berlin, and Stockholm. It is not because they naturally like the diet better, but because they would show that they belong to the civilized world, and partake of its culture. Not being able to do this at all seasons, they reserve it to be done when the season permits and trade is open. This is at least for three months in the year.

The Lord's Supper is a particular rite representing the communion of all Christians, and their partaking the benefits of Christ. Its form was prescribed by the Great Head of the Church himself—an infinitely greater than the source whence issue the formalities of civilized society. Shall Christians not show a zeal for conformity to what is the most proper form of the observance of what Christ has prescribed, equal to the zeal that imitates the capricious formalities that mark communion with the world of culture? The latter changes its forms every year; yet its votaries, even in Finland, try to keep pace with the changes. The rite that Christ ordained has remained the same through all the ages. It has been observed with worship of him by successive generations of his followers. It is simple in an extreme degree, and as much within the reach of all mankind as any device that could be imagined. As for the bread, it is as universal as the commerce of Christian nations. It may be had in the biscuit that every ship carries. Only the wine presents any difficulty. That, however, can be had at some season of the year by commerce. The expense is nothing to think of for a church, in the small quantity that is required. Let it be shown that people of the same degree as the Christians of any place cannot and do not procure tobacco and spirits from the temperate zone, before it is complained of as a hardship for Christians to procure wine, that with bread and wine they may observe the Lord's Supper in identical fashion with the rest of the Church of Christ throughout the world. It cannot be insisted on that the Lord's Supper should be observed as often as Christians would like to have it. There are churches where none of these difficulties are pleaded that think it expedient to celebrate the Lord's Supper only once a year.

What is now insisted on is important enough to make it an object. For Christians ought to feel no proper satisfaction in the Lord's Supper unless they can observe it just in that fashion that alone appears to be proper; and that ought to be just what Christians everywhere use. This must appear from consideration of the benefits of the Lord's Supper, which we must reserve for its appropriate place in this tract. One of these, however, is the sign-language involved in this ordinance. Many would justify the substitution of the common food and drink of the heathen for the bread and wine, as being a translation of this sign-language into the symbols of the region, just as they translate the word into the vernacular of the region. But precisely the opposite course is appropriate to a language of signs. It is meant for a universal language. We presume that Masonic signs, that are meant as the counter-signs for recognition and Masonic communion all over the world, are never accommodated to the conditions of different societies, but remain invariably the same. We all know what a tremendous barrier to Christian fellowship is found in difference of spoken language. Every Christian, in meeting Christians of a different speech from his own, feels the benefit of those words that Christianity carries with it into every tongue: Jehovah, Hallelujah, Baptism, etc., and, above all, Jesus Christ, the name that is above every name. By the sound of these they detect one another, and on that limited ground of common speech establish a communion. Two such Christians met on the same vessel in the Indian or some other ocean. In vain they tried to communicate. At last one exclaimed, "Jesus Christ!" and the other exclaimed, "Hallelujah!" and they clasped hands in a hearty relish of Christian fellowship. Any Christian can enter into the sympathy of such a scene. Imagine, however, two at the same table wishing to commune in Christ, but without a common speech. Let one take in hand bread and wine, and let the other extend his dulse and reindeer milk, and the sentiment of communion is confounded and wrecked as effectually as by the confusion of their tongues.

We are therefore constrained to differ from the view of this matter that has such respectable support as referred to above. We deny the fact of necessity that is pleaded for some countries to justify the substitution of something else for the bread and wine of the Lord's Supper. The latter can be procured, at some time or other, as easily as the presence of ministers, and Bibles, and hymn books, and places of meeting, and other things that are deemed essential to the existence of a church. During the time they cannot be had, the necessity should be accepted as exempting from the duty and the privilege of observing the Lord's Supper till the means can be procured for doing it in proper form; just as believers, living scattered and solitary, surrounded only by heathen, must wait till they can have opportunity of meeting together to celebrate the Supper. It is not the Lord's Supper if the elements are taken in solitude. Believers must, therefore, be at the cost and trouble of gathering in one place; the blessing of it is worth it. So Christians must accept the cost and trouble of getting the bread and wine in order that the Lord's Supper may be observed in its genuine form. Omission of the ordinance in this spirit would more honor it and maintain its integrity, and conduce to the preservation of a pure type of Christianity, than attempting the observance of the Lord's Supper in some mongrel form of substitution. If, in the church of Corinth, some believers refused to participate when the Lord's Supper was observed in that corrupt form that Paul censured, they more honored the ordinance than those who so pretended to keep it.

Next in order, *the wine claims attention*. Let it be remembered that we are considering what is the proper provision for the Lord's table, as it is spread for a meal, of whose provision all the communicants are to partake.

The wine has been the subject of prolific controversy in the Church. The greatest contest has been that with the Church of Rome, because she withholds the cup from the laity. In the Mass, only the priest drinks the wine of the cup; to the laity desiring to commune, he communicates only the wafer, which in that church is substituted for bread. For the laity, the cup, or chalice, is there only to be an object of adoration after the words of consecration have been spoken. It is elevated by the priest in the view of the worshipers, and they prostrate themselves before it as beholding the actual blood of Christ. This conflict remains unreconciled. Protestant Christians ought never to grow indifferent to it. Though the noise of the war of words may be suffered to die away, zeal for the true worship of Christ in this particular should remain, and the clear protest against the abuse of the Church of Rome be maintained with the same zeal that animated the Protestant Reformers. Such a protest is properly incorporated in our Confession of Faith: "The denial of the cup to the people ... is contrary to the nature of this sacrament, and to the institution of Christ. (Chap. xxix. § 4).

We are confronted at the present time with another conflict regarding the wine. Many insist that it must not be set on the Lord's table, and call for the substitution of something that is not wine—i. e., is not fermented juice of the grape. This movement is in the interest of the cause of temperance, and of resistance to the use of intoxicant drinks. It is not essentially a new controversy in the Church; it is only new as it appears in connection with the modern temperance agitation.

From the earliest period after the Apostles had been removed, the Church has been called on to decide again and again what that cup was that Christ gave to his Apostles, and they in turn to the churches; and in many instances the situation was so similar to the one now presented that, as to principle, they may be called identical. Cyprian (A. D. 258†) was moved to write a letter, because in some places Christians were using water instead of wine in the Eucharist. This, it is said, was not their uniform habit, but when they took the communion in the early morning, and was for fear the smell of wine should betray them to their heathen persecutors. Against this practice Cyprian protests with all authority, that it was a sacrilege perversely to make water of wine, when at the marriage feast Christ made wine of water.

Another sort of heretics were the Ebionites, sometimes called Encratites, and sometimes Aquarii, that is very much like total abstainers. Their total abstinence was founded on the erroneous principle that it was universally unlawful to eat flesh or drink wine. This error came from heathen sources into the Church very early, and lingered long before it was "purged out as an unrighteous leaven." We find it exposed and condemned in succession by Irenæus, Clemens of Alexandria, Epiphanius, Theodoret, and Chrysostom, not to mention more. The two last explain that those of this heresy substituted water for wine in the Eucharist. And Chrysostom says in refutation, "Because some use water in the mysteries [Eucharist] the Lord showed that when he appointed the mysteries he appointed wine, and when he arose from the dead and prepared his usual table, without the mysteries, he used wine. *From the fruit of the vine*, he says, 'Now the vine produces wine, not water.'"

Chrysostom, in commenting on Matt. 26:29, and by reference also to Acts 10:41, finds proof of his statement that Christ is expressly reported to have drunk wine after his resurrection, just as he ate common food.

The proceedings of the Third Council of Braga, Spain, A.D. 675, report: "We have heard that some schismatics offer milk instead of wine in the divine sacrifice; that others set before the people the bread dipped in wine instead of the complete sacrament; that others even offer in the sacrament of the Lord's cup wine pressed out of the clusters of grapes." (Bingham's Antiq. Bk. xv. ch. 3). All of which is mentioned only to condemn such practices, and to insist that the Lord's Supper shall be observed in exact conformity with what

Christ instituted and what had been traditionally observed, viz., by using simple bread and wine mingled with water.

The foregoing instances are sufficient. They show that we have no new phenomenon in the present desire to substitute something else for the wine the Lord appointed for his table. They show the same movement at very different periods, proceeding from various principles, yet always rebuked and condemned by the Church on the steadfast principle, viz., that Christ instituted wine, and that wine therefore must be used. They show, that if the effort to do away with proper wine in the communion should originate from any other imaginable motive, it must be condemned by the same inflexible principle. They show especially, that least of all can the cause of temperance present a motive for conceding what has been inflexibly refused to all other appeals; for from the foundation of the Christian Church this noble cause has been the cause of the best members of the orthodox Church. It presents no principle now that was not presented to the minds of the pious from the Apostles to the present time. The evils of intemperance have confronted the Church in essentially the same way from the beginning.

The Apostle Paul says: "Whereunto we have already attained, by that same rule let us walk." (Phil. 3:16.) As has been already said, if there is anything to which the Church can attain in doctrine and practice, that may be regarded as final—a thing ascertained, a question decided and not again to be opened, a principle of clear and inflexible application—then we have it, for one of them, in this rule, that proper wine is essential to the Lord's Supper. By that same rule, then, let all churches walk, as they would seek the unity, purity, and peace of the catholic Church.

If any suppose that the scruples that now lead some to use

something else than proper wine in the Communion are so respectable as to justify some concession, let them remember that very respectable scruples led to withholding the cup from the laity in the Romish Church. For that, as a chief reason, we are Protestants. The Reformation restored the cup to the laity; but if, having now the cup of the Lord, we change it from what he appointed it to be, we shall commit as great an impiety as that already committed by the Romish Church.

It is peculiar to the modern effort to change the wine of the Lord's Supper, that it attempts to justify itself by maintaining:

(*a*) That our Lord used the unfermented juice of the grape when instituting his Supper.

(*b*) That though he may have used wine—*i. e.*, the fermented juice of the grape—yet by the use of the expressions, "*this cup*," and "*the fruit of the vine*," he intentionally and providentially chose a form of speech that made the fermented quality of the contents of that cup he used a matter of indifference. Thus Christians are at liberty to use proper wine or not, so it be the juice of the grape.

The views just stated are originally and purely the inventions of the present generation. So far as we are aware, no one pretends to find a trace of them in any earlier age. It is even boasted that the foregoing ages were ignorant of these facts, and that it was reserved for this age to detect the truth in the light of history and providence. The attempt is made to establish a favorable presumption for these claims by appealing to the experience of the Church in regard to other things in the word of God. A later age has come to read passages of that word with a clear meaning that was unsuspected by preceding ages that read the same words. The most signal example is found in those words that express the great

Protestant doctrine of justification by faith, which before the Reformation were read without any apprehension of that sense. The appeal is not well made. There was no such absolute ignorance as the appeal assumes. But it is also a mistaken appeal, for the reason that the more enlightened reading of an age of the revival of religion and of learning had to do with spiritual facts—that is, revealed truth—and not with the facts of material living, and the doings of men. We cannot, at this distance of time, know what Jesus and his disciples ate and drank better than the men of their own generation and of the age following them. The amazing presumption of the present claim appears, however, in pretending to know better than Paul the Apostle what Christ drank at the Passover. For if it has been the mistake of the ages to suppose he drank proper wine, and gave that wine in instituting his Supper, Paul himself made that mistake, and was the most potent cause of its propagation in the Church. This will appear from what we have to say below.

But first let us detect wherein we stand on common ground with these innovators. It is significant that they deem it necessary to their justification to establish, that in using unfermented juice of the grape, they use just what Christ used. This involves the admission, that what Christ actually used when giving the cup, determines the meaning of his command when he said, "*Do this.*" If he used wine, then he commanded us to use wine. If he used the unfermented juice of the grape, then we are commanded to use that. In this position we are perfectly agreed. For our part, indeed, we strenuously insist on it, as the only way of knowing what our Lord commanded to be used.

The advocates of both (*a*) and (*b*), as stated above, find it necessary to disregard the deliverance of the Apostle Paul, in

1 Cor. 11, and make their appeal to the accounts of the institution of the Lord's Supper found in the Evangelists. We have shown above how this method is itself a violation of the Scripture. Nothing can be established about the Lord's Supper without 1 Cor. 11; and nothing can make it appear that Paul did not deliver to the Corinthian church that they must use wine. There the cup that was drunk was a cup of wine. From his words, it is evident that Paul understood that such was the cup that Christ used at first. He tells us that he gave the cup as he received the ordinance from Christ himself, and not as an ordinance received indirectly through the Apostles that were with Christ at the original institution. Thus, through Paul, the Lord reiterated his institution in the same form as at first. This has much the same assuring effect as identical testimony from two witnesses. For the same command was given at two distinct periods twenty or more years apart. This is proof that nothing in the lapse of time is to modify the observance of the Supper. And again, the same command was given to Jews in Jerusalem, and to Gentiles in Corinth—two great representative situations. This is proof that nothing in the varied conditions of nations is to modify the observance of the Lord's Supper. In all time, among all peoples, bread and wine are to be used.

Paul wrote to the Corinthians with the precise intention of distinguishing the exact and proper Lord's Supper from what was not that. What he delivered, therefore, is the exact and genuine rite; no more, and no less. And, moreover, the cause of temperance was conspicuously present in the distinguishing, and was a prominent matter. Let us say it was providentially there, in view of a period like ours, when that cause is justly made so great a cause. It was providentially there for an Apostle to deal with it in the authority that Christ gave him, in order to teach the Church of all time, both to set itself against intemperance, and yet to show that Christ's word and what he has ordained have an abiding importance that must be unaffected by the efforts to produce a reformation of intemperate customs. The Corinthians had been using wine to drunkenness; that is, some of them; and Paul denounced the sin, and meant to put an end to it, and to even the danger of it. But for that he did not change the wine of the ordinance. He appointed the Supper to be observed in a way that must preclude the danger of intoxication. They must have a cup out of which all were to drink; "the cup that is the communion of the blood of Christ."

This is more like providence than that to which innovators point. Providence provides for the future in the events of the past. These innovators find their providence in the events of the present, in the light of which they would change the plain meaning of Christ's words in the past, and transform the very facts of the past. We are founded in this matter of the wine on the Apostle to the Gentiles, and all that we know of the other Apostles only corroborates him. On this foundation we are built, and will be edified in a way not to be moved. And all who will confess to be of the Apostolic Church must stand in the same way.

It is needless, then, to follow the reasoning of those who would disregard the Apostle, and pretend to take their warrant for something that is not wine by consulting Christ himself as he is reported in the Evangelists. It is easy, indeed, to show to a fair mind, that when Christ said, "*this cup*," he as evidently meant the wine in the cup, as that the temperance orator of our time means by "the bottle," the spirits in the bottle; and to show that by "*the fruit of the vine*," he as clearly meant wine, as the same orator means spirits when he speaks of "the product of the still." But it is enough to observe that his Apostle Paul so understood the words and actions of his Master. This is interpretation that every one can understand, and needs no learning. Yet it is unimpeachable.

This movement against the wine of the Lord's Supper in the interest of the cause of temperance, is to be reproved and resisted as making the cause of temperance greater than Christ. We may illustrate this by what is understood in other things. The total abstinence cause has its sign. Murphy gives a red ribbon. In England, the blue ribbon is the sign of belonging to the ranks of abstainers. In Belgium, the red cross. In Philadelphia, the white ribbon has been adopted as the sign of the same thing. If this began with Murphy's red ribbon, no region is bound to adopt his ribbon. Another may be even better, just to show that it is not Murphy, but the cause for which they are zealous. The cause is greater than Murphy, and overshadows him. But such can never be the case with what Christ has instituted. There is no distinguishing between zeal for his cause and zeal for him. Salvation is the cause for which Christ came; but salvation does not overshadow Christ. What he has appointed as a sign, becomes in its use a sign of adherence to him as well as to the cause. To change that sign, as distinguishing the cause from himself, is a mark of departure from him. The Lord's Supper was instituted to show forth Christ, and it shows forth the cause by showing Christ. It is that by his appointment, and only serves its purpose perfectly when precisely what he appointed is done. To modify it on the demand of asceticism, or of total abstinence, so as to make it distinctively show forth those principles, is impertinence, intrusion, and presumption. It is all this as really as is modifying it to show forth the doctrines embodied in the Romish Mass. If, in a patriotic movement for political liberty, a badge and motto be adopted by the organizing head of the movement and given to all adherents, then only that is the unmistakable sign of the presence of that movement for liberty. Let there be made in any locality a change in the badge or motto, with the intention of identifying the cause of liberty with some matter of local interest, and the act would be treated as intrusion and presumption. It would be regarded as evidence that the local interest overshadows the national one of liberty; it would be suspected that the greater cause will be sacrificed to the limited one, and must expect no uncompromising and staunch support there. For experience teaches all this; and experience has taught the same in respect to loyalty to Christ. It is even the experience of the cause of Christ as related to zeal for total abstinence. When nominal Christians proceed so far as to say, that were they constrained to believe that Christ used wine and appointed it to be used by his disciples, they could not believe either in his goodness or wisdom, then it is evident that they make the cause of temperance overshadow Christ himself. And this rash and presumptuous saying has often been uttered.

Disregard of what Christ appointed is just ground for treating those who show it as breaking their relation with him. The Presbyterian churches so treat the Church of Rome for the changes it has made in the sacraments. Rome does not disguise the changes she has made, but maintains that authority resides in her, as in the Apostles, to make such changes. The effort to change the wine in the interest of total abstinence has nothing to redeem it from the charge of being as great an error as that of Rome. It is no redeeming trait that the innovators attempt to disguise the change by wresting the Scriptures. Wresting the Scriptures is as great a sin as Rome's presumption in usurping authority above them, to change what is there commanded. The only comfort about the newer error—*i. e.*, comfort for those who resist it—is that it is feebler in its devices for justifying itself. There is no great organized system lying back of the error to perpetuate it. It is simply a device for the occasion. When the fanaticism that prompts it wears away, the violence done to the Scriptures will be left in its naked deformity and loathsomeness, and the figment will be abandoned to contempt.

Proceeding with our main subject, which is to ascertain what is commanded to be observed as the Lord's Supper, *we are next brought to contemplate the actions proper to it.*

Action is the dominant characteristic of the ordinance. The command is, "*Do this,*" and Christ's actions on the occasion interpret the command. The attending actions lend the spoken words their true sense. Thus the action involved in the Lord's Supper is an essential part of it. This is true of it just as it is of any other meal, where the meal is of the nature of a feast which a host gives to his friends. This is our Lord's Supper, which he gives to his friends. The food that is provided at such a meal is not all of the entertainment, or even the most. The chief thing is the host, and the food is important only as his provision. The preciousness of the occasion is his giving it, and the guests receiving it so.

The Lord's Supper is to be observed in a manner that represents this giving on the part of Christ, and receiving on the part of his disciples. It is therefore to be observed in a form as representing a transaction. Not reproducing in a spectacular way a transaction that occurred long ago, but a transaction actually taking place. This is intimated in what we accept as the Apostle's directory for this act of worship. It is obviously not Paul's purpose, in 1 Cor. 11, to give the history of the original institution of the Lord's Supper. There is nothing to indicate that his readers did not know that history. It is to be assumed that they did. They commemorated it. But they did it in a faulty and gross way. Paul corrects them by reminding them how he had delivered the ordinance to them. He did it by reciting what he here again repeats, and with the few words he ends, as having perfectly represented how he formerly delivered to them the Lord's Supper, and as having sufficiently directed them how to do. There is something abrupt and incomplete in this for the present reader The reason is, Paul assumes that the Corinthian readers will recall with these words his appropriate actions on the occasion referred to. When he delivered an ordinance like this, it could only be by the actual observance of it. It needs no proof that when Paul delivered the Lord's Supper anywhere he administered the rite. His words in 1 Cor. 11 recall his actions to the minds of the Corinthians on that occasion when he delivered the ordinance to them, and he repeats only the words of the institution as he used them; this was his directory for them; and it is the same for us. It is easy to see how completely it corrected the gross manner that some had used. They mingled the eating of bread and drinking of wine for the Lord's Supper with gluttonous feasting. "When ye assemble yourselves together it is not possible to eat the Lord's Supper. . . . For as often as ye eat this bread and drink the cup ye do show the Lord's death till he come." What is described in the latter sentence is incompatible with what is referred to in the former, viz., such assembling as the Corinthians observed. And the *"for"* of the latter sentence, like the *"for"* of verse 21, is to introduce a reason why such meetings could not be the Lord's Supper. According to verse 21, it could not be the Supper by reason of what *they* did in eating. According to verse 26, it could not be, by reason of what the real Supper is when properly observed.

We see, then, that the Apostle's directory represents the proper action for the Lord's Supper. It is to be administered as the Apostle administered it, reciting the story of the original occasion, and speaking the words Christ used at the original institution, accompanying all with appropriate action. Such is the mode prescribed in our Directory of Worship, which permits the words of the institution to be repeated as they are found in 1 Cor. 11, or in the Evangelists.

The action appropriate to the administration of the Lord's Supper consists of the simple motions that Christ himself used. He took the bread—*i. e.*, a loaf—and gave thanks, and brake it, and gave it to his disciples to eat. Likewise he took the cup, and gave thanks, and gave it to his disciples for them all to drink of it. While doing so he said of the bread, "*This is my body, which is for you;*" and of the cup, "*This cup is the new covenant in my blood.*" And of each he said, "*This do in remembrance of me.*" Speaking these same words is essential to the action of the observance.

The corresponding action on the part of the recipients consists of the same simple motions that the twelve used when Christ gave them the bread and wine. They are simply, as at a meal, to receive and eat the morsels of bread, as all partaking of the one loaf, and to drink the wine, as all sipping from the same cup.

With this simple ritual the observance of the Lord's Supper is complete, according to the directory of the Apostle. Our Directory for Worship prescribes very properly, that the service shall close with a prayer, followed by a hymn, and the benediction that dismisses the congregation. These parts, however, belong to what is proper to every religious assembly.

The usage is the more precious and suitable for this solemn observance, because the breaking up of that original company, when Christ instituted his Supper, was attended with the same acts of worship. Christ prayed, as recorded in John 17; and we are told that, "*when they had sung a hymn, they went out unto the Mount of Olives.*"

We notice that the directory of the Apostle omits the mention of Christ's returning thanks when giving the cup, of which fact we have account in Matthew and Mark. Luke in this corresponds to 1 Cor. 11. We may infer that Luke's account is determined by what he heard so often from Paul, as the latter often in Luke's presence administered the Lord's Supper. The difference we note is naturally accounted for when we reflect, that Paul's recital was not for historical purpose, but for actual administration of the Lord's Supper. In the original Supper an interval occurred between the giving of the bread and the placing of the wine—an interval variously employed. This made it expedient, as it was also the custom at the Passover Supper, that when the cup was introduced, the solemn thanks should be repeated. But in the observance of the Lord's Supper in the churches, the cup follows immediately after the bread has been received. The act of returning thanks would naturally be for both at once. This is an adaptation that an Apostle might introduce; and such authority is warrant enough for the Church now to use the same observance. It cannot be deemed improper should any prefer to introduce the cup by a second act of prayer. But neither is it improper to omit that, according to the Apostle's directory. It is important, however, that celebrants should know the true ground for the omission by them. It is not the obvious expediency or propriety of one act of thanksgiving for both the bread and wine, because both are present. It is the Apostolic example of direction that is the warrant. The difference between Matthew and Mark on the one hand, and of Luke and 1 Cor. 11 on the other, in the matter of the blessings, is no discrepancy. It is not doubtful whether Christ twice gave thanks, and thus a matter of liberty whether in our celebrations thanks shall be given twice. Had we only the accounts of Matthew and Mark for our direction, we should be bound to give thanks both for the bread and for the wine. But having the Apostle's precise directory, we are justified in giving thanks only once.

It is involved in the foregoing recital that one should be the minister for all the rest, and represent Christ in these actions and spoken words. It is essential that this should be a minister properly ordained and charged with this duty. But the reasons for this latter being essential do not belong to the Lord's Supper itself. The Lord's Supper is something of itself, just as Baptism is, and as ordination to the ministry is, and the gospel itself is, and membership in the church also. The proper ministry by which these things are administered is something distinct, and thus, when it is our purpose to consider only the Lord's Supper itself, we may omit the consideration of the ministry that is essential to the proper observance of it. To a foreigner wishing to become a citizen of the United States, we may explain what citizenship is, without explaining all about the process of naturalization; though without receiving the latter through the proper officers, he can be no citizen.

We have now represented the essential parts of the Lord's Supper according to the only directory that can be recognized as of catholic authority. Thus we have answered the question, What is commanded to be observed? The sum of it is as follows: The Lord's Supper is to be observed by congregations of believers assembled for worship. It is a meal to be eaten together by them, without combining it with any general eating. It is therefore to be set forth as a meal, its provision being placed on a table decently set before the congregation who are to be supplied from it. The proper provision of the Lord's table is bread and wine; the bread being common bread, whether leavened or unleavened, and the wine being common wine. One, and a properly qualified minister, is to dispense the provision in the name of Christ and as representing him. He does this using such simple actions as Christ used in doing the same. He takes the bread or loaf, and giving thanks, breaks it and distributes it to be eaten by the believers present, saying, "*This is my body.*" And likewise he takes the cup, and giving it to be drunk by the believers present, says, "*This cup is the new covenant in my blood.*" These the believers present are to recieve and eat and drink as at a meal, only so that they eat as all eating of one loaf, and drink as all drinking from the same cup.

We maintain that all that is commanded in this simple ritual is easily understood, and as such is to be scrupulously observed with exact conformity. *When so observed, that is the Lord's Supper.* Wherever it is so observed it is easily and instantly recognized as being what Christ appointed, and it achieves what it was intended for: it shows forth his death. It is to be perpetually observed in this way in order to show forth his death till he come.

HOW WHAT IS COMMANDED IS MISUNDERSTOOD.

As a matter of fact, however, what is so simply commanded has not been understood by many. In other words, it has been variously understood. As a consequence, the Supper is so variously observed that it is sometimes impossible, without explanation, to recognize as the same thing the different ceremonies that claim to be the Lord's Supper. This obliges us to *consider the process by which what is in itself so simple of understanding is made difficult.*

We have noticed (page 13) one of the ways in which many confuse their understanding of what is commanded. They assume that the essential thing in the Lord's Supper is receiving the grace and benefit it is intended to convey. Hence they infer, that where such sanctifying benefit has been experienced in observing the Lord's Supper, there the Lord's Supper has been essentially observed. We have shown that this affords no clue to ascertaining what is essential to be observed as the Lord's Supper, from the very nature of the thing appealed to, and from the fact that God often attends the faulty use of the means of grace with a blessing. Moreover, we have shown that it is unwarranted to assume that all the blessing of the proper observance of an ordinance has been received because some grace has been received. There may be, and we believe there certainly is, much that is missed when the observance has been imperfect. Joash, at Elisha's command, smote the ground with arrows. "He smote thrice, and stayed." According to that symbolism, he received a blessing of smiting Syria so as to humble it. But that blessing would have been no proof that he observed all that was essential to the symbolism the prophet intended. The prophet was there to reveal his fault and its consequences. "The man of God was wroth with him, and said, Thou shouldest have smitten five or six times; then hadst thou smitten Syria till thou hadst consumed it; whereas now thou shalt smite Syria but thrice." (2 Kings 13:18, 19). If it be assumed that the essential thing about the Lord's Supper is receiving the grace it confers, then the question, What is commanded in the Lord's Supper? becomes an inquiry, How shall I obtain the grace that the Lord's Supper conveys? Then

Christ's command, "*Do this,*" is understood to mean, Seek this grace. This leads to the belief that there is a grace attending that ordinance that the believer can get by no other, and it is called sacramental grace. This is all confusion, which we need follow no further. It is all of their own making who use this method of finding out what is commanded to be the Lord's Supper. Where one's attention is simply directed to celebrating the Lord's Supper so that it shall evidently be that identical institution that Christ gave his Church, there can be no confusion about what is commanded.

Another way in which men confuse their minds about what is commanded, is by assuming that the essential things in the Lord's Supper are the truths it signifies; whereas, the essential things are the signs that Christ appointed to signify the truths. With this assumption, however, it is inferred that only those traits of the Supper are essential that symbolize such truths. It is an easy step from this, not only to neglect parts that are not recognized as symbolizing anything, but also to adopt the use of other things that seem as well fitted to symbolize the same truths. Viewed in this light, the question, What is commanded? becomes exceedingly perplexing; and the answers to the question become as various as the fancies of different men; for when it comes to interpreting symbolism, fancy has very full play. By this method of interpreting what is commanded, the symbolism of eating bread is taken to mean, that as bread is the staple food to support life, so receiving and appropriating Christ is the support of eternal life. What is commanded, then, is not to eat bread, but so to eat as signifying that we derive our life from Christ. The bread, then, is not essential. That was the staple diet of Palestine, an accident of Christ's environment. The staple diet of another region is rice, or perhaps fish. For such regions, then, these may be used, and the essential feature of the Lord's Supper be still observed. So also of the wine. It was the accident of that occasion when Christ instituted the Supper. Unless in the fermented quality of the wine there can be detected a symbolism essential to the Lord's Supper, it must be deemed unessential. Then the unfermented juice of the grape is as proper as the fermented; and where wine is not the common drink of the region, whatever is the common drink will do as well. It is obvious that this method of ascertaining what is commanded to be observed in the Lord's Supper can only result in confusion and difference. This should be enough to condemn it as an error. It is precisely in this way that most of the divisive controversies about the Lord's Supper originated.

We are saved from all this when we accept the ordinance of the Lord's Supper from the Apostles, as the institutions of others are received by such as recognize their right to devise and appoint them. The Congress of the United States adopts a flag, and appoints it for the flag of the country. There is a symbolism in the stars and stripes. But those who use the flag do so, not because they recognize the symbolism, but because that flag has been appointed and is the flag of the country. Let any one say, "It does not matter whether the red or the white stripes have the larger number. Thirteen red and white stripes is the essential symbolism, or, indeed, thirteen stripes of any kind," and he does as those do who would determine what is commanded in the Lord's Supper by referring to what is signified instead of to what is commanded. Let one unfurl a flag with the red and white stripes in a different order from that adopted by Congress, then his flag is not the flag of the United States. However insignificant the difference may appear to some, there are situations where it would be of great importance. It would be just where it is all important that the flag should be the flag of the United States. The would-be flag displayed on the seas in time of war would not be respected even by a United States cruiser. It is in time of peace, and in mere parade, that a faulty flag of this sort may be tolerated. There is reason for thinking that those who change the signs that Christ appointed are making parade and play of Christianity.

The original Passover was to be observed by sprinkling the posts and lintels of the doors with blood. At that and the annual Passover observed in succeeding ages, the lamb was to be chosen four days before it was killed; the lamb was not to have a bone of it broken. Had those who were commanded to keep the Passover used the above erroneous method to ascertain what was commanded, they would have neglected these things, for the symbolism of them was not detected. But they used no such method. They took what was commanded simply, as a child takes the word of its parent. They scrupulously observed the ordinance. Down to the time of Christ, the lamb was killed and eaten without breaking a bone of it, without the meaning being suspected by a single worshiper. But when Christ died on the cross, without any breaking of his bones to hasten death, then the significance of the old symbolism was revealed. "For these things came to pass, that the Scripture might be fulfilled, A bone of him shall not be broken."

In the same way we receive a command to observe the Lord's Supper; and what it is, is plainly set forth. Our part is scrupulously to observe it as commanded. It is a monument like the Passover, that points not only backward, but forward. It is essential that the monument be maintained precisely as it was instituted. The rule of exact preservation is not found in our intelligent reading of its signs. Some of the signs may have no meaning to us. Some may not even attract our notice at all as signs, any more than the unbroken bones of the lamb attracted the notice of the Israelite. Yet those very signs may, by the events of the future, appear in glorious prominence and significance. As for the wine so much in dispute, what if we can see no significance in its fermented quality? It is especially to the wine that Christ gives a peculiar significance connected with the unknown future. " I will not drink henceforth of this fruit of the vine, until the day when I drink it new with you in my Father's kingdom." (Matt. 26:27.) What that means remains an impressive mystery. It will remain such till Christ comes again, and actually drinks the wine new with us: new, not as meaning fresh juice of the grape, but new in a similar sense to the new in the new covenant which the wine now represents. With that before us, it is our duty scrupulously to use the wine as the new covenant in his blood, till he shall come again and change its use into the significance of a newer and still more blessed dispensation.

The manner of distinguishing between the accidents and the essentials of the Lord's Supper, already referred to, is also one of the ways men confuse the question, What is commanded to be observed? It assumes, indeed, to be the very opposite, and is supposed to be the very method of clear logic for avoiding confusion. It deserves the more serious and careful examination for this very reason; for if it be an error, or if it be only a correct method erroneously applied, the error is a fundamental one of far-reaching effect. It has actually been used to the utmost extent of its application in scholastic philosophy. As much as anything else, that logical method is the characteristic of scholasticism. On no single subject has it been used with more adroitness and effect than on the Lord's Supper itself. It is by that method that scholasticism supposes it can establish the reasonableness of the doctrine of transubstantiation. By that method it would persuade men that it is no affront to the understanding to maintain that what the senses tell them is bread and wine, has been transformed into the very body and blood of Christ. This is warning enough that any use of this method to ascertain what is commanded is attended with the peril of sophistry, if it be not itself essentially and altogether sophistry.

Shall we consider the bread and wine the mere accidents of Christ's environment? Shall we reflect that had he been in India he would have used rice and toddy? Or shall we say of the bread, that at least its unfermented quality was an accident; and of the juice of the grape, that its fermented quality was an accident, and treat as unimportant what we so discover to be accidental? How many other things, then, about the sayings and doings of Christ were accidents? How much of Christ himself was an accident? Following this clue, the cross was an accident. Had Christ appeared in Rome, he would have been thrown into the arena to the savage beasts. This leads up to the notion of an "Oriental Christ" for Orientals, and a Western Christ for Westerners. These things are no more accidents (we mean in the philosophic sense) than the facts that Jesus Christ is the seed of Abraham, and that salvation is of the Jews. They are essential to Christianity, which is the "great mystery of godliness: he who was manifested in the flesh, justified in the spirit, preached among the nations, believed on in the world, received up into glory. But the Spirit saith expressly, that in later times some shall fall away from the faith, giving heed to seducing spirits, through the hypocrisy of men that speak lies; commanding to abstain from meats which God created to be received with thanksgiving by them that believe and know the truth. For every creature of God is good, and nothing is to be rejected, if it be received with thanksgiving; for it is sanctified through the word of God and prayer." (1 Tim. 3:16; 4:1-5.) This saying of the Apostle came early to pass, and such falling away from the faith has been often repeated. One special and very effective form of "the hypocrisy of men that speak lies" has been this method of ascertaining what is commanded by distinguishing the accidents from the substance of the command. This "leaven of hypocrisy" works mightily now in the lump of nominal Christianity. "Let us keep the feast, not with old leaven, neither with the leaven of malice and wickedness, but with the unleavened bread of sincerity and truth." (1 Cor. 5:8.)

Jesus Christ, of the seed of David; crucified by the malice of the Jews at Jerusalem, under Pontius Pilate, a Gentile governor; preached to the nations by Apostles of his own sending—all this, with all the particulars that belong to the several parts, are essential to Christianity. They go where the gospel goes, and are essential to salvation, as leading men to trace their redemption to that grace of God promised through Abraham and given to the world through that redeeming work of Christ which he accomplished at Jerusalem in the land promised to Abraham. Nothing is merely accidental in all this, either in the common or in the philosophical sense. The cross was no accident, nor giving Jesus vinegar to drink, nor parting his garments among his executioners, nor casting lots for his vesture, nor leaving his legs unbroken, nor piercing his side with a spear. When the Scripture expressly forbids our treating these things as accidents, we have reason enough for being careful how we treat anything that Christ said or did or suffered according to this method of distinguishing the accidents from the substance. If there still be something correct that underlies this method, such as distinguishing between the form and the spirit, let us seek a correct expression for it.

We maintain that the bread and wine the Apostles gave the Church are essential to the Lord's Supper, simply on the ground of their being plainly commanded. We may, however, follow the suggestion that comes from this attempt to make them appear unimportant. Granting that they have a particularity that is derived from the time and circumstances of their original institution, we can as well see in that the marks of their importance as of their unimportance. These temporal and local features are of use to manifest and maintain the truth of the historical connection of Christianity with Christ and the land of Canaan where he wrought the work of redemption. There is reason enough to preserve and make the most of anything that properly serves such a purpose. Never was there an age when there was more reason for this; for the present time, more than any previous time, is characterized by insidious efforts to make Christianity an abstraction. The most popular form of this effort, at the present time, is the attempt to divest it of all that is local in time and place, and doing the same with Buddhism and other religions, to discover the one universal religion that belongs to all time and to humanity everywhere. All this, then, presents just so much the more reason to the true Christian for holding tenaciously to the observance of everything in Christianity that evidences its origin as derived from Christ, and as identified with the promised land, and the promise to Abraham that in his seed shall all the nations of the earth be blessed. Let us be thankful, as for the good that appears where evil is intended, that by the very method that would render the wine of the Lord's Supper of little or no importance, we are led to see an importance belonging to it that has been much overlooked. Let us scrupulously observe the

Supper as the Apostles gave it, that it may bear the clearest marks of its origin both as respects time and circumstances. Thereby (without any expedients or inventions of our own, which are to be sedulously shunned) we will set forth Christianity in its distinctness from all other religions, and proclaim it and profess it as the only religion that offers salvation to the world.

The above caution against using our own inventions is needed. Christian churches are ever making greater account of such things than of matters of actual divine appointment. The Church of Rome gives the most striking illustration of the importance there may be in holding tenaciously to the marks that manifest and maintain Church identity. There can be no Roman Catholic Church without a priest and the sacraments of that church. But the priest is no priest without ordination issuing from Rome through a bishop consecrated at Rome; the bishop is no bishop without his ring received from the Pope; nor the archbishop an archbishop without his pallium; all this in order to manifest and maintain a vital, organic connection with Rome and the visible head of the church. This every Romish church shows. It involves great trouble. But grant that the Roman idea of the Church is correct, and all this is essential, and not the least thing may be omitted. The Church of England, for the same reason, holds it essential that the Book of Common Prayer shall be used for worship in all its churches and missions, that their identity may appear, and how they derive their origin from England. In Presbyterian churches the Westminster Confession of Faith serves the same purpose. By nearly all churches it has even been recognized as important that the church bell and steeple should go wherever the Christian Church goes, to be marks of its historical derivation and identity.

All these things have their importance and are essential in their way. But this only shows how, for reasons founded in human customs everywhere, the very circumstantials and so-called accidents of the sacraments that Christ appointed have their importance, and thus are essential to the proper observance of these sacraments. Let us be zealous for the things that mark the denominational identity of churches; but let us be more zealous for the scrupulous preservation of those marks about the Lord's Supper that stamp it as derived from Christ and from the land of promise, where "he died for our sins, and rose again for our justification." Here is a matter where must be applied the saying of Christ: "These things ought ye to have done, and not to leave the other undone."

What we contend for is, that we have a ritual in the directory of 1 Cor. 11; for such is the issue of all that we have so far been representing and defending. What we contend for in regard to the Lord's Supper is a strict and scrupulous adherence to the letter of the ordinance as received from the Apostle in 1 Cor. 11. The result is imitation; and in effect we maintain that it is imitation of the Apostle's way of administering the ordinance that is enjoined on us. This imitation as proposed to us in his directory is extremely simple. It does not call on us to notice anything peculiar to the manners of the table either in Jerusalem or Corinth. The directions we have studied were applicable to every situation where Paul planted a church. Without the slightest change in the directions, the customs of any place would either fit the occasion or be adjusted to it; the latter more frequently; but how little adjustment for a ceremony so simple! The same would be true of all times and localities.

Both the things just stated—a ritual, and the obligation to observe the very letter of it—may seem very objectionable to some. It may be supposed that these things conflict with the very spirit of Reformed theology; and, as that theology studies to represent a pure Christianity, the meaning would be, that they conflict with the spirit of Christianity. It may be objected to what we represent, that Paul says, "We are ministers of a new covenant, not of the letter, but of the spirit; for the letter killeth, but the spirit giveth life." (2 Cor. 3 : 6.)

But first, as to this particular Scripture, it is evident that by "the letter," Paul means the written law of the Old Testament. This appears from his contrasting with it the "new covenant," and saying we are ministers of that, and "not of the letter." It appears further, in that he explains his statement, "the letter killeth," by using as its equivalent in the following verse the expression, "the ministration of death, written and engraven on stones." And in all the other places of his using the same expression, he means the same thing. (Compare Rom. 2 : 27, 29; 7 : 6.) It is therefore not a principle stated in abstract form that we have in the above words of Paul concerning "the letter." It is a concrete thing, viz., the old covenant, as a bond written in ordinances, that was against us (Col. 2 : 14), to which he opposes the new covenant, which we have in the forgiveness of sins through Christ, who has taken away the other, nailing it to the cross. He means the commandment which he "found to be unto death." (Rom. 7 : 10.) This, indeed, involves a principle of general application; but the Apostle does not make the general application in the places where he uses the expression. Reformed theologians usually make this general application, and very naturally use the Apostle's expression to state it. But that statement and his must not be confounded. The Apostle's statement is no authority for presuming that we must find no rules and prescriptions attending the new covenant that are to be obeyed to the letter. As a matter of fact, we find several matters of ritual, and the Reformed theology not only recognizes them, but is the foremost advocate for a scrupulous and exact observance of their letter. Baptism is one, which, to be Christian Baptism, must be with water, applied to the subject, with the use of the prescribed formula. Ordination to the gospel ministry is another, which must be observed with laying on the hands of Presbytery. And one day in seven to be a weekly Sabbath is another. The Lord's Supper is another, which, to be the Lord's Supper, must in some respect or other be observed in a Scriptural form. The only question is, What is that Scriptural form? We believe that our Directory for Worship, in requiring the form for which we contend, presents that Scriptural form. We have shown that it is precisely that form that the Apostle directed to be used.

The form in all these things is just the essential matter, when they are regarded as observances that we must keep. The identity of what we do with what the Apostles did, and commanded us to do, must be seen in the correspondence of our form with theirs. As regards the Lord's Supper, no one ever doubted about the bread and wine that was approved as proper in the church of Corinth, until the temperance zeal of the nineteenth century instilled the doubt into some minds respecting the wine. The Apostle sanctions the use of the fermented juice of the grape, the wine of common life in the regions where the churches were first planted. We know perfectly well what wine is, though we may be perplexed to know whether something offered to us is really wine. These two things are not to be confounded. The latter difficulty neither makes the former perplexing, nor does it justify the notion that it is a matter of indifference whether we use wine or not in the Lord's Supper. Some presume to say that these particulars, and scrupulous adherance to them, are to our Lord only as "mint, anise, and cummin." Let them remember, then, that our Lord said of those that displayed their zeal by tithing such things, that they ought not to leave such tithing undone. (Matt. 23 : 23.) Their fault was not their conscientious application of Lev. 27 : 30, but their neglect of the weightier matters of the law. But when it was wine that our Lord used, and that his Apostles delivered to the Church to be the emblem of the new covenant, it is disobedience to use anything else, or to regard it as anything but a "weighty matter." To urge that it is significant that Christ and his Apostles say "the cup," and do not expressly mention the wine in the cup, is subversive of all interpretation. What shall we say of baptism? *Baptizo* is used of Christian Baptism commonly without express mention of water. In reference to John's baptism, the water is expressly mentioned in eleven out of thirty-five instances of its mention—quite enough to show that water was essential to his baptism. But in the twenty-eight instances of the mention of Christian Baptism, water is only twice expressly referred to. In these instances we find six that reiterate the statement of the Baptist: "I baptize you with water, but he shall baptize you with the Holy Ghost and with fire." (Matt. 3 : 11 ; Mark 1 : 8; Luke 3 : 16 ; John 1 : 26 ; Acts 1 : 5 ; 11 : 16, and add Acts 19 : 3–5.) One other mentions impressively that Jesus himself did not baptize (John 4 : 2), and another that Paul declares to the Corinthians that Christ sent him not to baptize, but to preach, and that he did not baptize many. Is the absence of express mention of water with baptize in Christian Baptism significant? May we infer that the water is not essential? May sand answer as well? or breathing or fanning to signify the baptism with the Spirit? or some device of fire to signify the same thing more impressively, because more dangerously and extraordinarily? or shall we infer, as the Quakers do, from just such Scriptural evidence, that the sacrament of Baptism itself is unessential to Christian worship? The last mentioned inference comes sooner or later, when men begin to treat with contempt the scrupulous observance of what the Apostles delivered to the Church, just as they gave it. It proceeds to the neglect of all sacraments and ordinances, and ere long issues in irreligion. History abundantly confirms this statement. What else is to be expected? Where so simple a command as "Do this," which plainly means, "Give and receive bread and wine according to Christ's appointment," can be distorted to mean, "Do not do this," it will be much easier to mystify men's minds about the words that teach us to believe Christ's doctrines, and distort them to mean, "Do not believe them."

In all that has so far been said, we have, in the interest of defense, noticed various ways in which the simple ordinance of the Lord's Supper, as delivered by the Apostle (1 Cor. 11), has been changed. This has led us in the same connection to point to the evils attending such departures from strict conformity to that directory. *These changes come about by ignorance of what is the Lord's Supper; or they are urged as the necessity of the situation of some Christian churches; or they are made deliberately and of design.*

The mildest form of such error is when it is the result of ignorance. The ignorance may be excusable, but it remains ignorance; and the effect of it is, that such faulty observance of the Lord's Supper becomes a display and monument of ignorance of what the Head of the Church instituted to be a most signal mark of his Church. Where there is such a display of ignorance in a matter so central and important, there is reason for inferring serious ignorance about the whole subject of true religion. Such persons cannot perpetuate pure Christianity. Their case is like that of the disciples Paul found in Ephesus. They used a baptism, but it was not Christian Baptism, because it lacked the essential feature of reference to Christ. Therefore Paul baptized them unto the name of the Lord Jesus. Let a man display a flag of stars and stripes as a sign of his being a citizen of the United States, and able to represent the nature and advantages of citizenship in the United States; if it be discovered that the flag is not the true flag, men may justly infer that, as he does not know the flag of his country, neither does he know the country he claims to represent.

Where error in the mode of observing the Lord's Supper is excused on the ground of necessity, because the proper bread and wine are not to be easily had, we have maintained that the plea is not to be admitted. As the ordinance may not be observed unless there be a company of believers (if it be but two or three met in the name of Christ) to make a communion, neither let it be observed till that company procure bread and wine, that they may break the bread that is a communion of the body of Christ, and bless the cup that is a communion of the blood of Christ. Or if any substitute be used, let the effect attach to the whole ceremony, and call it all a substitute for the Lord's Supper, and forbear to call it the actual Lord's Supper. The question of such an expedient might be entertained; but we are sure it would have little interest; for no church, however small or poor, would rest content with a ceremony that is merely a substitution, and is disowned as the right and proper observance of the Lord's Supper.

Where the change made in the Lord's Supper is deliberate and designed, there the error is a much more serious thing. There we have not longer to consider what may be the hurtful effect of the faulty observance of the ordinance. The situation is reversed, and we see in the change the evidence of harm already done. The question then becomes, What has happened that men presume to change the ordinance of the Apostles? The answer, first of all, is, There has been a departure from Christ. The changed observance is itself the sign of that. The Romish Mass is a monument of departure from Christ and the Apostles. It does not serve to commemorate the death of Christ on Calvary, or to exhibit the covenant of grace in Christ's blood through that one sacrifice for sin that he made when he offered up himself. However these may find expression in the prayers of the Mass, that few of the worshipers hear, the ritual overbears them all, and sets forth a present and actual sacrifice for the worshipers to contemplate, and the work of the sacrificing priest at the altar as the work that procures remission of sins. These changes, and all that belong to them, are the effect of an antecedent departure from the true doctrine of justification by faith in Jesus Christ alone. They are the effect of the visible, organized church usurping superiority above the Holy Scriptures, and claiming itself to be the repository of Christ's authority, and of the grace of salvation.

And wherever else changes are made in the Lord's Supper deliberately and by design, it is the sign of antecedent departure from Christ and his Apostles. We have pointed to the evidences of this in those who would change the wine of the Communion cup. It may be urged, that if such substitution be an error, it should be referred to the head of ignorance. This may be allowed in the case of those who have been brought up in such ignorance. Even then it can only be allowed just as we allow it in the case of Roman Catholics who have been born and brought up in their error. But there is no room for such allowance in the present matter. This innovation is too recent for us to treat any as having been brought up ignorantly under its influence. It has not yet educated a generation; but many of our generation have been departing from the true obedience of Christ and his Apostles.

BENEFITS ATTENDING THE PROPER OBSERVANCE OF THE LORD'S SUPPER.

We may now give attention to what is the most grateful part of the task we have proposed in this tract, viz., the consideration of *the benefits attending the scrupulous and exact observance of the Lord's Supper as delivered to us by the Apostles.*

We would have it noticed, that we have been treating our whole subject in that simple order presented in Question 96 of the Shorter Catechism. Up to the present point we have considered what may be comprehended under the clause: "The Lord's Supper is a sacrament, wherein by giving and receiving bread and wine according to Christ's appointment." We now enter upon what may be properly comprehended under the subsequent words: "His death is showed forth, and the worthy receivers are, not after a corporal and carnal manner, but by faith, made partakers of his body and blood, with all his benefits, to their spiritual nourishment and growth in grace."

We would call attention to the characteristic of this method of contemplating the Lord's Supper. It is, that we first ascertain what is the ordinance—in other words, what is commanded—with the simple purpose of doing as we are commanded; and then we seek to know what is the benefit attending the thing commanded.

The comparative excellence of this method of inquiry deserves some special remark. Our question, What is the benefit attending obedience in this matter of the Lord's Supper? appears to be substantially the same subject as that commonly proposed under the heading, "The design and significance of the Lord's Supper." They ought, in fact, to be the same subject. Our question, however, approaches the investigation in a different fashion from the other. We have learned already that this may not be a matter of indifference; for we have observed that the other method leads those using it to determine what is commanded by what they suppose is signified and designed. This may seem to be serving "in the spirit and not in the letter," and to be agreeable to what Christ said of the relation between himself and his disciples: "The servant knoweth not what his lord doeth; but I have called you friends." But we may press too far the notion that we know what our Lord does. It is pressing this too far, when we assume that we know all that he intends by something he commands us to do. We press it to sinful presumption when, supposing we know his intentions, we change the doing of what he precisely commands, with the idea that what we do equally achieves his intention. It was such presumption in Peter when he supposed he was only using proper friendly liberty in saying once to Jesus: "This be far from thee, Lord." It would have been such presumption in those disciples whom Jesus sent to procure the ass for his triumphal entry into Jerusalem, had they procured some other, because more convenient, or perhaps nobler beast, in the belief that they knew their Lord's intention. It would have been the same, had those who were to prepare the Passover, done so in some other room than the one they found by following the precise directions that Jesus gave them, in the belief that the particular room was not essential. Let us remember, that in the same room, and at the same supper where Christ said: "I have called you friends," meaning that a friend knows what his lord does, he also said of something he was doing: "What I do thou knowest not now; but thou shalt understand hereafter." This is as much the description of the disciple's relation to his Lord as the other. One must not be taken and amplified without the other. He said the latter with reference to the simple ceremony of washing the disciples' feet, which, when he resumed his seat, he immediately proceeded to explain and make them understand. Very few moments after, he instituted the Lord's Supper, telling his disciples to observe it. They did not know then what he was doing. It was not till after his resurrection that they knew, what they then delivered to the Church, viz., that this Supper is to be observed till Christ shall come again. But now knowing that, we may not assume that we know all that Christ does by the observance as it is perpetuated. We must assume, rather, that we know not now, but are to understand hereafter; perhaps at the period he indicates in the words: "I shall drink this fruit of the vine new with you in the kingdom of my Father." As long as we are ignorant of anything he may propose by this Supper, we have no liberty to do anything but to observe it in strictest conformity to the direction he has given us. When we have done what is commanded, we are in the best situation for contemplating the benefits intended by the ordinance.

Such, then, is the advantage of the method we use, in preference to that which asks first, and as if before compliance, What is the significance and design of what we are commanded to do? Different methods often have very different results, even when they seem very nearly the same. The method we use has the sanction of the Great Teacher himself, for he says: "He that doeth the truth, cometh to the light." Different methods indicate difference in the spirit of inquiry. The method we discard has much of that querulous temper exhibited by children who ask "Why?" before doing what they are told to do.

It is common to treat scrupulous obedience, and strict regard to the letter of what is commanded, as something slavish, and opposed to a free service in the spirit. But there is no incompatibility between adhering to the letter and a free service. The assumption that there is, leads many to act and speak as if nothing may be regarded as a duty that has no other claim than simply that it is commanded. The same persons, when maintaining that something is a duty, are apt to enforce it by all sorts of considerations except that which is the first, and of first importance, viz., that it is commanded. In regard to the Lord's Supper, however, it is evident that we observe it because it was appointed. Obedience is our first action in the matter, and we must study to make it exact obedience. Our first inquiry, then, is:

What benefit attends this act of obedience to Christ?

There is benefit and blessing attaching to all obedience in general, and this general benefit must not be overlooked in this connection. But we inquire now, What is the peculiar benefit attaching to this particular and singular act of obedience? It is unlike the obedience we generally render to God's will; for in general we obey as led by the Spirit, the form of the action being variously modified by ever changing conditions, so that sometimes the believer seems inconsistent with himself. Thus Paul sometimes used circumcision, and sometimes not; sometimes ate meat offered to idols, and sometimes severely refused to do so. With the difference of form the spirit remained the same. In observing the Lord's Supper, however, we obey as performing a precise thing, continually and often repeated in the same fashion, according to precise directions transmitted to us from Christ himself.

The benefit of this obedience attaches exclusively to the fact that what is done is commanded by Christ himself, and is so transmitted directly to us. This directness, however, depends entirely on the performance being precisely what he ordained. Every change, either of omission or addition, impairs the directness and immediateness of what we receive. Let one find an ancient coin, fresh and unworn, the image and superscription in sharp relief, and he feels that he has it fresh and directly from the mint. It is as if coined that very day. In studying it, time and use and change do not come in as factors. Few ancient things come into our hands in that condition; when they do, it is because they have been unused. The Lord's Supper, however, was appointed for use, and can only be preserved by use. But it is one of those things that may be used without wear or change. When we observe it as commanded, we do just what the disciples did with the Apostles on the day of Pentecost, and for precisely the same reason. This obliterates time and history in our relation to Christ, and brings us into close and even almost visible and audible relation to him. It is like the sealed orders that a naval commander opens and reads when he has got out to sea. It is then as if he had that very day been in the Navy Department and taken his commission and orders. He executes the orders in that spirit, reading and interpreting them in their own original sense, unaffected by any words, events, or current news that have come to him since the sealed orders were put into his hands. So, when observing the Supper according to Christ's command transmitted directly to us, and not as conforming to the custom of the society to which we belong, or heeding anything said or done in our environment, or coming to us from any antecedent conditions, we feel and manifest in the clearest way possible the immediateness of our relation to him. We show our faith in him, our assurance that he lived to give the command we execute, that he lives to witness our obedience, and to requite it. In all this, as obedience alone, apart from the intelligence we have of the import and effect of what we do, we have a most precious and necessary benefit of personal closeness to our Saviour, and apprehension of him as "The captain and perfecter of our faith." (Heb. 12:2.)

In urging these considerations we appeal to a sentiment that is universal and well appreciated in other matters dear to men's hearts. This is the sentiment that devotes to historic use the chamber in which a great man died. The clock was stopped at the moment he breathed his last; the bed remains as made up for him to lie on; the furniture is preserved exactly as he used it, with the various matters of his latest employments displayed as if he were just gone out from being occupied with them and must soon come back. Many a home has such an historic chamber, that is meant in the same way to cherish the feeling of the nearness of some departed parent, wife, husband, or child, and preserve the freshness of their memory unaffected by the changes of time. Time seems to be shut out of such places, and only now remains. It is not always pleasing to witness such things. But the only just ground of disapproval is the apprehension that there may be idolatry in the sentiment; as it is evident there often is. But that which is the danger where we oftenest see this sentiment gratified, only shows the fitness of using the sentiment where there can be no idolatry. If it be so effective as to betray us into idolatry of the cherished objects we mourn, it will foster in our bosoms the adoration of the Saviour we worship. Let us, then, give it the best application by directing our care to the observance of the Lord's Supper in such a fashion as is now contended for. We will thus take our directions from Christ himself, and, forgetting time and change, we will feel the nearness of him who is yesterday and to-day and forever the same. We are at his table who said: "A little while, and ye behold me no more; and again a little while, and ye shall see me."

All this precious benefit is marred and the effect weakened if, instead of such precise execution of the original directions, we do something that is a modification of them, whether derived from preceding ages through which the institution has come down to us, or occasioned by conditions peculiar to our own time and place. Just in proportion as these modifications are allowed, what we do affects our souls with the sentiment of a Saviour known and followed afar off; followed at the distance of intervening centuries, and commanding us through the medium of expression as changeable and indistinct as language itself. Instead of the signet ring, received direct from the hand of the king himself, with its device well defined, and its mounting uninjured, and its jewel bright and flashing, we receive it worn and inarticulate, and its jewel scratched and dimmed, and are left to apprehend that its original virtue as the king's signet may have been withdrawn.

Let no one imagine that this benefit of obedience, to which we are pointing, belongs necessarily and only to the simplest believers, because of their want of intelligence as to the meaning of what they do, and their small attainments in Christain knowledge. It is an error to suppose that this posture of the believer toward the Lord's Supper may be surmounted and lost sight of in the superior benefit of a more intelligent observance of the ordinance. For believers of the highest attainments, this benefit of implicit obedience will still remain the primary and necessary benefit; for it is still true of them that they do not know what Christ is doing in this observance that he instituted. After all that they have learned to know, there is more that they cannot know, and will not understand till hereafter. A docile disciple should take this for granted, and as of course, without needing the confirmation of experience —in other words, of history—to assure him of it. And such a disciple will, consequently, as little presume to change the ordinance of the Lord's Supper from what Christ gave, as the most ignorant disciple. He would say: "I do not know what I may be doing in making the least change. I will not wittingly make the slightest change. To do so would be a forwardness and presumption like that of Joseph, when he attempted to change the hands of Jacob from where the Patriarch had laid them on the heads of Ephraim and Manasseh." It is precisely such forward presumption when persons of our time justify a modification of what the Apostles delivered to the Church as the Lord's Supper by saying: "If our Lord had lived in our time, he would not have sanctioned the use of wine."

But if this scrupulous regard for what was transmitted to us for our observance be not learned from the instincts of proper docility, let it be learned from experience; take the lesson from the history of controversies about the Lord's Supper. All this controversy, that has filled more books than any other, may be traced, as to its chief cause, to men's assuming that they know all that the Lord intended by this ordinance. According to this assumption, they have modified the ordinance to make it exhibit their notion of its meaning; and the controversies have been about such changes and the doctrines involved in them. The controversies, then, show that men cannot agree as to what the Lord intended by his

Supper; and this is a practical confession that what he does we know not now. There can be no such controversy about what his words by the Apostles prescribe, if we read them without presuming to interpret them by their intention as derived from the significance of what he would have us do.

Let the Lord's Supper do what it was intended to do; or, better stated, let our Lord do, through his Supper, what it is his purpose to do. That must be by our observing it just as he commanded, and in simple conformity to his words. That ordinance has, perhaps, yet a long history before it. Let us transmit it by our custom just as it has been transmitted by the inspired Scripture. Let us attach no modification to it that must remind our posterity that it has come to them through the medium of our local conflicts or transient enthusiasms. History proves that the power of Christ's presence with the Church has been in proportion as this ordinance has been preserved in its purity according to the Apostolic directory. The history of the Reformation in the sixteenth century affords most striking illustration of this. If not, then Church history can teach nothing, and we may despair of interpreting providence.

We feel assured that where a believer's posture toward the ordinance of the Lord's Supper is that for which we contend with so much reiteration, and where he is sensible of that benefit of strict compliance that has just been represented, his mind will be disabused of the perplexity many feel regarding what is commanded. Instead of objecting that all this is true of what is commanded, but that the question of what *is* commanded is untouched, he will see that the simple course is to do just as the Apostles did, and that imitation is obedience, and obedience is imitation.

Let us now proceed to consider another benefit attending

scrupulous compliance to the letter, in observing the Lord's Supper as the Apostle delivered it. Observing the very letter belongs to the very spirit of such an ordinance, seeing it is a divine ritual. This one is essentially a letter, for it has a meaning, and that meaning is most exactly preserved and expressed in the letter.

We have, then, the benefit of a universal and imperishable language of signs. In the benefit first dwelt upon, we have regarded the letter only as expressing a command, in order to represent the precious effect of exact obedience. This was treating the things prescribed to be observed as something sovereignly and arbitrarily appointed by Christ; which indeed they were. But this does not exclude their having a fitness and propriety in themselves. It is only in the case of mere men like ourselves that we dissociate arbitrariness from fitness or reasonableness. Thus, to say a command is arbitrary, is to intimate that it is unreasonable, or has no inherent propriety. It is, however, to be assumed that whatever Christ appoints will in itself be reasonable, and have a deep fitness and meaning. It ought equally to be assumed that whatever he appoints to signify anything is the very best device for the purpose.

The Lord appointed his Supper to proclaim his death. It holds up to view his death as the paramount fact concerning him and what he did. He is to be remembered ever after as having died. What he is, as remembered and preached to the world, he is by virtue of that dying. He is the Saviour, and he saves by his death. This is the foundation truth of redeeming love. His blood is the new covenant of the remission of sins. His body is given to us to be our life. His actions in this ordinance, while handling the elements, signify his imparting himself and all his benefits to us. Our actions signify our receiving them. *Thus we have, in the language of signs, a repre-*

sentation of the most essential truths of the gospel; the truths which, if received and held sincerely, are sure to bring with them all the details of saving knowledge, as preached by the Apostles, and as they are still to be preached wherever the gospel is carried.

This truth Christ preached himself in words, and committed the words to them that heard him. But in the form of words alone it was committed to a changing medium of expression. The tongue in which Jesus spoke is no longer a living language, and his very words in that tongue were not to be preserved in written documents. Languages, even when living, undergo change, and the expression of the same thought in the same language must be modified accordingly. The expression in the original form becomes obscured by the newer modifications of meaning in the terms used. It requires learning to interpret what was said so long ago in an archaic form of the language. How much more obscured is that which is expressed in a language now dead! It is evident that it is important, if possible, to express the truth that is for all time and peoples in a language that cannot change, and that will be equally expressive to all. This our Lord did by the appointment of a few simple symbols to be a language expressive of himself and of his message to the world he came to save. By a few words, capable of exact translation into any language, he weds to these signs a clear and fixed meaning. The language then devised speaks to all. As long as the signs are repeated just as they were given, the meaning they express is the same.

This language of signs in the Lord's Supper is not exposed to change and modification as human speech is. If change be made, it is by design, and not by reason of a law of development, such as appears in speech, and is the proper study of philology. This symbolism is the language of Jesus himself. When reading the Gospels, many a Christian has wished for the impossible, viz., that he might himself hear the Lord speak. In the Lord's Supper, however, our Lord has achieved the impossible. He has made it possible for every disciple of his, till he shall come again, to have the essential truth and the sum of saving knowledge expressed in his Lord's own language; a language as expressive and clear and unmistakable as when it was first uttered. This utterance does not die away in echoes. It does not become confused in sense. We receive the communication just as the twelve received it in that upper room in Jerusalem. It has none of the obscurities of spoken language, that needs the tone and emphasis of the living voice to give it the exact interpretation. It is not confused by ambiguities of grammar that attach to spoken language when reduced to writing. It is not exposed to change or mutilation, as written language is by transcription in manuscripts. The signs are simple, and so few, and so easy of exact reproduction, that nothing can be omitted where there is real intention to repeat them. When so reproduced, they say just what Christ says. Not a few, when contemplating that wonderful modern invention, the phonograph, have wished that some such appliance had taken up some of the words of Christ just as he uttered them, and made them accessible to a listener now. Ah, how great a price of admission would be paid now to hearken to the faint mutterings of such a recorder! It would be treasured as the chief oracle of Christendom. The infallible Pope would be insignificant compared to it. But in the Lord's Supper, Christ has contrived such a record of his message to the world he came to save. He makes ourselves part of the language, so that, as we observe the Supper in simple obedience and faith, we cannot but hear and understand.

All this is a very precious benefit attending the scrupulous and exact observance of the Lord's Supper. It is obvious that, such as it is, with its necessary conditions, this benefit is forfeited when believers permit modifications and changes in the observance of the Supper growing out of the various conditions of times and places. In proportion as this is allowed, the language of these signs becomes confused and confusing. As the telephone sometimes brings to the ear of the listener, not one distinct message from the person with whom he wishes to communicate, but a confusion of utterances caught from various contiguous wires, so these symbols of the Lord's Supper actually come to the communicant in the Romish Church, not with the simple message received direct from Christ, but with a confusion of utterances contracted through a long course of history. These, and especially the voice of the church claiming to be the dispenser of saving grace, drown that message that Christ himself wedded to these symbols. If in any other form we had a discourse of Jesus, a parable even, though brief as that of the mustard seed, a record in the very language he used, with the modulations and exact emphasis of his voice, who would dare to treat a single feature of it as unimportant? Who would regard lightly the slightest obliteration, or even change, of it? Would not every jot and tittle of that be as sacred as every "jot and tittle of the law"? And what a strange obliquity it is, when Christian scholars devote prodigies of talent and labor to the task of settling the genuine original text of Scripture, and the same scholars deem it of little importance whether that symbolical language be tampered with which Christ gave his Church, and by which he gives his own expression of the doctrine of salvation through him! Let us, as we would for ourselves hear our Saviour himself speak to us the truth of salvation and the assurance of our part in its benefits, preserve the uncorrupted text of that language in which he expresses it. And as we would obey his command, "Go ye and make disciples of all nations, teaching them to observe all things whatsoever I commanded you," so let us use in uncorrupted purity that universal dialect through which he would communicate with his disciples of every tongue under heaven, and himself point them to his death as the price of their redemption. This will promote the communion and the real union of believers over the whole world, and the Lord's Supper will be, as it is meant to be, the sign of a Church that has one Lord, one faith, and one baptism. As a matter of fact, notwithstanding the faultiness with which the Lord's Supper has been so often observed, church history shows that this institution has contributed mightily to preserve in the world the belief and confession of the fundamental truth of Christianity, that sinners are redeemed and saved by the death of Christ, the Son of God.

We have now considered two great benefits attending the scrupulous and exact observance of the Lord's Supper as delivered by the Apostle, viz., the benefit of this formal and peculiar act of obedience, and the benefit of having the precise form of symbolism by which Christ communicates his saving truth to the world he came to save. We call these primary benefits, because they are the first and preliminary benefits connected with the ordinance; just as in learning a science, the preliminary condition is to possess for use a correct text book of instruction, and the first benefit is the actual possession of such a book. This primary benefit is not the chief benefit of the Lord's Supper to those personally who observe it. Though the simple act of obedience by which the ordinance is preserved and perpetuated has, indeed, a great importance and benefit in itself as regards those who are to receive it from us and as regards what Christ intends to effect by it till he comes again, yet even all that benefit must fail by an observance that rests in and is satisfied with the form alone. *It is in the significance of the Lord's Supper that the chief benefit is found by those who observe it.*

Therefore, *we must now contemplate the meaning of the expressive language of signs appointed in the Lord's Supper.*

The same scrupulous care is to be observed in regard to the meaning we receive, as in receiving and observing the form. This language of signs, though faultless in itself, may be faultily interpreted, just as spoken language is faultily interpreted by repeating it with an accent and emphasis of parts of it that was no part of its original expression, and as written language is misinterpreted by reading between the lines. The symbolism our Lord adopted is sufficient for all he meant to express. As we are not to change the signs he gave, either by addition or omission, in order to make them signify what they did not signify as they were delivered, so, too, we must forbear lending to them a redundancy of expression. There is a purity and majesty of style in this kind of language as well as in speech. It appears in simplicity, directness, and strength of expression, as opposed to effort and straining after richness and variety. It is the Doric form of architecture as compared with the florid and overloaded creations of barbaric taste. The symbolism of the Lord's Supper is the former. Men who mistake multiplicity and variety for strength of expression, as much wordiness is often mistaken for wisdom, would make of it the latter.

As an example of corrupting the simple majesty of Christ's own expression, may be mentioned the significance that some attach to the water mingled with the wine. If there was such mingling of water with the wine our Lord used, as it is reasonably certain there was, it was simply due to custom, as the same has always been usual in countries where wine is produced and is the drink of the people. It still leaves the drink wine, as much as it is wine by the original making, which is often attended with some mixture of water in the wines of inferior quality. What our Lord gave when appointing the Supper was wine, and the water mingled with it was not singled out for any significance. To that wine he wedded one meaning. It is the blood of the new covenant. Those who would find in the water a symbol of the water that issued from Christ's side with the blood, when his side was pierced, find a meaning that the Lord did not express. And when they mingle the water with the wine by a distinct ritualistic action, they add something to the Lord's Supper that was not appointed, and that is a transgression of the command, "Do this."

Another example of corrupting the simplicity of expression of the Lord's Supper, is where men borrow from the sentiments prevalent at common feasts of food and wine, and single out the stimulating and joyous effect of wine as intended to be an expressive sign. There is nothing in any inspired account of the Lord's Supper to call attention to this.

Another example of the same sort is where the entire ordinance is interpreted in that fashion that is supposed to be the origin of the theological, but not Scriptural, name of sacrament. Borrowing from the ceremony of a Roman *imperator* mustering in the soldiers of his legion by an oath sealed with blood, Christ is represented as binding his followers to his service by a covenant of blood in this ordinance. It is supposed that this interpretation is justified by the expression, "This is the new covenant in my blood." Being intended as a proper interpretation of an essential part of the Supper, this representation is to be treated with respect. It is nevertheless an uninspired invention, and an addition to the meaning intended by the ordinance, and imposed upon it.

Still another example of the kind is where the meaning of the Lord's Supper is summed up in the expression, the Eucharist. As a name for the ordinance, this is as old as the Apostolic Fathers. Its origin is very natural and simple. It is like that name, "the breaking of bread," for the same thing, that we find in the Acts of the Apostles. As the latter was derived from the simple ceremony of breaking the bread, or loaf, in the Lord's Supper, so the former was derived from the simple action of giving thanks, for it is the Greek word for thanksgiving. As at first used, it is an appropriate and beautiful name. But when, as early came to pass, the name is transferred to the bread and wine, and these are then contemplated as an offering to be made with thanksgiving, and the whole ordinance is so observed as to be a ceremony of worship and praise expressive of thanksgiving for Christ's redeeming work, this is completely to miss the simple meaning of the Lord's Supper, and to pervert its intention and use.

There is, fortunately, a natural process of self-correction attending the use of such terms, that sometimes, though not always, divests them of their fanciful meaning, and leaves them with a proper one. By this process, sacrament has become a proper theological name common to both Baptism and the Lord's Supper; and Eucharist has been left a good name for the Lord's Supper, to signify that it should be observed with thankfulness, as attended with the blessings for which we pray when giving thanks at the beginning of it.

The examples just given of redundant and trivial interpretation of parts of the Lord's Supper, are not intended as condemning all use of such sentiments in connection with the ordinance. These, and others like them, may be properly taken in a suggestive way from the matter of the Lord's Supper to enliven meditation on it, and to impress the lesson of duty and devotion proper to be considered when approaching or leaving the Lord's table. But let all such sentiment be strictly marked for what it is, and refused as interpretations of what the Lord's Supper was meant to signify. From the parable of the leaven, one may take occasion, from the fact that leaven commonly symbolizes corruption, to impress a lesson about the ruinous effect of admitting even a little corruption into one's life; as Paul says, "A little leaven leaveneth the whole lump." But it would pervert the import of the parable itself to try and find room for that symbolism of leaven there.

Where there is an effort to detect all the possibilities of symbolic meaning, and gather them into a bundle of varied expression, real sense and meaning is overwhelmed and lost. An illustration of this effect, in a different way, is afforded by the habitual punster, who is ever on the lookout for the possibilities of double meanings in the words of others. The turns of sense and subjects brought about by such ingenuity make serious discourse, with earnest and direct meaning, impossible. So one may deal with the symbolical matter of an expressive though simple ritual in a similar way, till the excess of varied meanings confounds all direct and truthful sense, and issues in pious frivolity. Thus, the strained effort to make the most of everything, ends in making nothing of anything.

The benefit of the benefits so far mentioned—*i. e.*, the benefit of scrupulously obeying the ordinance concerning the Lord's Supper, and thus of having Christ's message in the language in which he expresses it—*is in the meaning or truth expressed.* The value of this is the measure of the value of the benefits already mentioned. If that meaning were of little value, the obedience by which we secure the exact expression of that meaning would have little reward.

Turning, then, to seek the meaning of the Lord's Supper, *we find ourselves contemplating a transaction.* The meaning is in all of it. This is needful to bear in mind. By doing so we will escape the error of supposing we find all its meaning concentrated in only a part of the transaction. This mistake is easily made. We may look only at the bread and wine, and see significance only in them. Were we to hear Christ speak, we would give exclusive attention to his words, as if his whole meaning were in them; as it would likely be. So we might suppose, when he gives us bread and wine in the Lord's Supper, that all the meaning is in them. This would be a mistake. Men, however, have made this mistake, and have sought all the meaning and benefit of the Lord's Supper in the bread and wine alone. They look for Christ's presence, and they find it in the bread and wine. They seek participation in the life of Christ, and they regard the bread and wine as imparting that. They seek the forgiveness of sins, and they must use the bread and wine in procuring that. By natural progress from the mistake of finding all the meaning in the bread and wine, there was evolved the Romish doctrine of transubstantiation, according to which the bread and wine become the very body and blood of Christ. Thus he is conceived to be present in those elements. Thus partaking of those elements is conceived to be essential to partaking of the life of Christ. Thus it is supposed that those elements must be offered up by a priest as a sacrifice to make expiation for sins. It is evident how important it is to contemplate the whole transaction of the ordinance as the language whose meaning we are to understand.

Contemplating, then, the transaction, *the first and supreme thing of all to be noticed is the presence of Christ himself.* The transaction represents that Christ blesses and breaks the bread, and gives it with appropriate words to the receiving believer; and in like manner he gives the cup. The Reformed churches have scrupulously observed the custom of requiring the minister to adhere to the precise words of the institution, and to act as imitating the actions of Christ, in order that the observance may represent that. It is not permitted to appear as if the minister or a priest gave to the communicant the body and blood of Christ. *In this transaction is expressed the presence of Christ objectively and really.* At the Lord's Supper, Christ and his disciples are together.

How can this be? A very natural question, just as natural as the same inquiry by Nicodemus regarding the birth from above. But we are not required to know or say *how* it may be. Jesus did not tell Nicodemus how a man is born again, except to say that it is the work of the Holy Spirit. That a man must be born again to see the kingdom of God, we know on the authority of God's word, especially as made plain in Christ, the last agent of revelation. And what we are to know in the Lord's Supper is, that Christ *is* present. Of that we can only be assured by himself. He has given his Church this assurance when he said, "*Lo, I am with you alway, even unto the end of the world.*" The presence of which this is the assurance, is the same that is enjoyed in the Lord's Supper; for where he is present with his Church, the whole Christ, the Son of God and the Son of man, is there. It is only on the ground of his personal assurance that we can know that Christ is present. That assurance may be given in various ways. It was given to the disciples by his visible, bodily appearance, as he came after his resurrection, "and stood in the midst of his disciples, and said unto them, Peace be with you." (John 20:19.) He gave it again in the parting words quoted above. That assurance remains with us. He gives it again in the Lord's Supper by expressive signs appointed to signify it. Of the two forms of this assurance left with the Church, that one last named, the Lord's Supper, is the superior. This superiority does not consist in expressing the truth more clearly, nor in being more reliable, nor in better revealing *how* Christ is present. But being the language of action, that also involves the believer in action with Christ, the truth expressed by it, that Christ is present, takes hold of the believer's apprehension with conviction in a way superior to the power of an assurance in words uttered long ago and reported by others. For this effect, however, the transaction which is the expressive language in this matter, must be such that the language is Christ's own, according as we have previously contended. As this condition is secured by the obedience of faith, the believer is thereby rendered worthy and fit to apprehend the presence of Christ, and to feel the power of the assurance thus conveyed.

When we sift the notion of presence, and separate it from the *conditions* of presence, that vary with different things, we repose more easily in the assurance of Christ's presence. We confuse our thinking, and thus our apprehension of presence, by confounding the conditions essential to the presence of one thing with those essential for another. Most things must be near us in space, and have always the same form or quality as apprehended by the senses, for us to be assured of their presence. The untrained judgment of a little child depends on such things in order to be assured of the presence even of its parent. Let the father go away full-bearded in the morning, and come home in the evening close shaven, and his little children will likely treat him at first as "company," as one testifies was his actual experience; and he had difficulty making them know that he was father come back. The little children need to learn to recognize a parent's presence by a different order of evidence from that which suffices for a dog or cat. So the believer needs to learn to know the presence of Christ by a different order of evidence from that which is the condition of a merely human presence. We have learned to apprehend the presence of the sun in the earth, in its noontide light and heat, though the sun is millions of miles distant in space from the earth. And, to use an illustration of Dr. A. A. Hodge, the man who, while standing on the Jersey side of the Delaware, heard Whitefield preaching at the foot of Market street in Philadelphia, was as really present at that sermon as the people that stood in Market street; and Whitefield was really present with him. "If another person is only one foot distant, but separated from you by a wall which cuts off all light and sound, he is as absent as if in the centre of a distant star." (*Lecture on Theological Themes, p.* 409.)

These observations are not made as if they helped us to get nearer to understanding *how* Christ is present at the Lord's Supper, or at any other time. But they divest our minds of the feeling that the conditions essential to presence of other things are essential to his presence. What the conditions essential to Christ's presence are, we cannot know. We only see that as they need not be those that we observe in other things, so they actually are not the same. We learn that the atmosphere is essential to the effective presence of the sun as we observe it on our globe. Outside of that atmosphere the presence of the sun must be a very different thing, both as to light and heat. We learn, also, that faith in us is essential to our effectively apprehending the presence of Christ with us. "Faith is the assurance of things hoped for, the proving of things not seen." We have assurance of Christ's presence, by faith in the various expressions and evidences he gives of it. Among these the Lord's Supper is the most assuring, from the nature of the expression of it. It is not expressed particularly by the bread and wine in our hand, and appropriated by us. It is expressed by the whole transaction of the ordinance, as a language by which he presently speaks to us with clear and unmistakable meaning the truth of his salvation, and communicates to us himself and all his benefits.

The presence of Christ in the Lord's Supper, as expressed and assured to us in the ordinance itself, *is the same as his presence with the twelve when he instituted the Supper*. It is the same presence, with the difference of his not appearing visibly to the eye and sensibly to the touch and hearing. A vast difference, indeed! Nor have we the least interest in disguising or slighting the magnitude of the difference. We may even find interest and satisfaction in giving the difference its fullest effect, as the best way of disabusing our minds of the feeling that his presence and identity can only be recognized by the evidence of the senses. We may do so, not as feeling that this is the best we wish for; for we desire to see Christ; nor as pretending that we understand why it is best for the present situation that we should not see Christ's presence. Paul saw him after other disciples had long ceased to see him. We do not know why it might not be good for Christ to appear to some others in the same way, if not to all disciples. For then, on their testimony, as by Paul's, we should have a most assuring evidence of his presence with his Church.

The situation as it is, however, has its compensations. It shuts us up to the necessity of recognizing and identifying the presence of the Lord in things of nobler quality than bodily shape and conditions of space. Men and women have often seen their beloved ones so changed and disfigured by disease, or so mangled and misshapen by accident, that they have had to identify them in defiance of all the evidences of the senses. The unfortunates can, indeed, be present still only by the conditions essential to material presence. But the shape, the voice, the expressions and gestures are all changed. These could not be more different from what they were, were they those of a totally different and unlike person. Yet those that love them identify them. The identification is the recognition of the spirit that animates that misshapen body, and speaks in that strange voice, and expresses itself in those unfamiliar gestures. The same personal presence is there, and is identified and loved and cherished. Yes, and the person is cherished with greater affection, because in a more noble and exalted love in the spirit. There is a compensation felt in realizing that our knowing one another attaches to something more than what the senses help us to. The spirit expresses itself through signs and gestures and tones of voice that would revolt the beholding friends were it another spirit that manifested its presence and meaning thus. But now they contemplate the changed expressions with compassion, and attend to them with joyful eagerness, as the only medium by which they feel that dear presence and receive its communications. The evidence that it is the same presence is the spirit of the man that speaks to them, and the spirit of the man in them that apprehends another human spirit. "Who among men knoweth the things of a man, save the spirit of the man which is in him?"

"But we have the mind of Christ," "And no man can say that Jesus is Lord, but in the Holy Spirit." By the Spirit of Christ dwelling in him, the believer recognizes the presence of Christ. He manifests himself, indeed, in the Lord's Supper in a form strangely changed from that in which he appeared on earth. "He hath no form nor comeliness; and when we see him, there is no beauty that we should desire him. He was despised and rejected of men; a man of sorrows and acquainted with grief." But this came about by no accident, nor by disease. "He was wounded for our transgressions, he was bruised for our iniquities; the chastisement of our peace was upon him; and with his stripes we are healed." But through the medium of the changed expression we recognize the personal presence of our Lord, and attend with eagerness to his communication. We are not revolted at that body that was crucified, and pierced by a spear. We do not shudder at that blood streaming from his hands and feet and side. He does not expect that of us. It is just those things he communicates, that we may have communion in them. Thus he signifies that he imparts himself and all his benefits to us. And we receive the bread and the cup for what he would have them signify, while in our inmost heart we say, "Unto him that loveth us, and loosed us from our sins by his blood; and he made us to be a kingdom, and to be priests unto his God and Father; to him be glory and dominion forever and ever. Amen."

In the words of the institution that the Apostle gives us, the transaction is introduced by the words: "*The Lord Jesus, the same night in which he was betrayed.*" *These brief words sufficiently set the scene for the action.* It was while the treachery of Judas, in combination with those who sought to compass the death of Jesus, was actually at work and near the moment of success. All was known to Jesus. He took that time, in full view of his approaching death, to institute this ordinance for his Church. The repetition of these words, as often as disciples begin to celebrate the ordinance, sets the same scene again. It is into that environment that the communicants are introduced, and there they meet with their Lord. It is obvious that the presence of a table spread with a promiscuous diet, and even the nearness of such a feast, as something just dispatched, is wholly incompatible with such an environment. This preface, then, both reproved the faulty observance of the Corinthians to whom Paul wrote, and guards believers for all subsequent time, as it ought already sufficiently to have prevented the Corinthians, from observing the Lord's Supper in any light and frivolous way. In what a light of self-forgetfulness, of love, of providence, and of self-sacrifice this scene, so set, presents our Lord! It is well summed up in the words with which the Beloved Disciple prefaces his account of that, to him, never-to-be-forgotten evening; "Now, before the feast of the passover, Jesus, knowing that his hour was come that he should depart out of this world unto the Father, having loved his own which were in the world, he loved them unto the end."

The transaction that takes place in the Lord's Supper is between Christ and his disciples. While the transaction itself gives the assurance of that which we must regard as the supreme thing of all, viz., the presence of Christ, it does this just by reason of the fact that *he does something* in the Lord's Supper. *In representing the benefits of the ordinance, we must consider Christ's part in the transaction, and then the believer's part.*

"*The Lord Jesus took bread; and when he had given thanks, he brake it, and said, This is my body, which is for you: this do in remembrance of me.*"

Such was *our Lord's action* in using the bread. Taking the bread and giving thanks was an action by which he appropriated that bread to the sacred use which he was instituting. "*He gave thanks*" is an expression denoting that act of worship in receiving food wherein thanksgiving is rendered for the gift of food, and prayer is made for a blessing on its use. The action denoted that he was about to use the bread for food. It teaches that in doing the same thing, as he has appointed, his disciples are to make the occasion one of thanksgiving for the gift received, and of prayer for blessing on its use. It is not a mournful transaction, this solemn Supper, but a thankful feast. As such it is a privilege to be admitted to it.

It was a loaf that our Lord took, and having returned thanks for it, as for food, *he brake the loaf* into fragments, to distribute it among his disciples. The Apostle recites only "he brake it, and said, This is my body, which is for you." So the Revised Version of 1881 gives the text, according to the consent of the majority, and, indeed, of almost all of the latest critical editors. If this be the correct text, then the action of breaking the loaf, is the process of reducing it to fragments to divide it among those that are to partake of it. Then the words of the Apostle are sufficiently explicit to denote that Christ gave of the bread to the disciples, though he omits the " and gave," that we read in Matthew and Mark. Accepting the text thus commended to us, we see that the meaning of breaking the loaf is that the disciples were all to partake of it. To this meaning Paul emphatically points in 1 Cor. 10: 16, 17, "The bread [loaf] which we break, is it not a communion of the body of Christ? seeing that we, who are many, are one bread, one body: for we all partake of the one bread." In all these mentions of "bread," the correlative expression in common English is "loaf."

We are thus taught that there is a meaning in the action by which one loaf is divided among all present so that all eat of it. This is communion—*i. e.*, partaking in common, and all alike. The communion in this instance is not *with* Christ; though there *is* a communion with Christ. But this is communion of the disciples *in* Christ, by altogether receiving what Christ communicates. Taking of one and the same loaf represents that there is a oneness or unity in them. What the nature of that oneness is, is represented by the loaf. It first of all means that all are one loaf, or bread.

But our Lord attaches its peculiar meaning to the loaf. He said, "*This is my body, which is for you.*" Knowing, as we do, that the presence of Christ in the Lord's Supper is the same as his presence with the disciples in the first Supper, we will view the bread and wine to be used just as they did. We will, therefore, no more mistake his meaning than they did when he said, "This is my body," "This is my blood." With Christ personally present in bodily shape, and speaking to them, and in action with them, they could not take the idea, any more than they could conceive the possibility, that that loaf he held in his hand, or the fragments of it that each received, or the wine of which each supped, was changed into the substance of Christ, so that the bread was his very flesh, and the wine was his very blood. Neither could they take the idea that his presence then or thereafter was to be identified with those elements particularly and exclusively. Our Lord said of the loaf, "This is my body," meaning that it represents his body; as his name, Jesus, represents his person. In the same sense he says, "This is my blood."

We observe that the text commended to us by such weight of scholarship omits the expression so familiar to all Christians, "This is my body, broken for you," and reads simply, "This is my body, which is for you." Accepting this text, it follows that the breaking of the loaf has no meaning in addition to that already dwelt upon, as if it also symbolized the violence done to Christ's body in crucifying him. The reluctance with which we part from this interpretation of the action of breaking the bread is relieved by considering the disadvantages attending the long received reading. As a symbolic action, the breaking of the loaf is not obviously fitted to represent a violent death, or even dying at all. Moreover, when confronted with the fact so solemnly emphasized, that, like the Paschal lamb, not a bone of Christ was broken, it has a conflicting sound to say that his body was broken, even though the word be taken to express only the violence and excruciating anguish inflicted on that body. Were we even to adhere to the long received text, it were better to understand the "broken" as referring only to the loaf as appointed to represent the body of Christ, and to communicating that body to believers. This meaning has been contended for quite apart from the question of the text, and long before attention was generally called to that. With this view of the meaning, Paul is left to say no more than the evangelists when giving the report of Christ's words. With the more common view, he appears to report what they omit.

What Christ says of the loaf is, "This is my body, which is for you." He says it of the loaf. Of the fragments into which he brake the loaf, it is true that each is his body, but only as it could be said, This is the bread that was in Christ's hand. The language of Paul quoted above, "We are one bread [loaf], one body," fastens our attention on the loaf in Christ's hand. Giving that loaf to his disciples represents giving his body to them, which is giving himself, that they may partake of him, and imparting his life to them, that he may be their life. Jesus had taught his disciples in a way to prepare them to apprehend his meaning in this action. "He that eateth my flesh and drinketh my blood hath eternal life. . . . He that eateth my flesh and drinketh my blood abideth in me and I in him." (John 6 : 54, 56.) In this action he represents the same truth. But he does it now by giving in emblem his body, not particularizing flesh and blood, because he reserves the blood for another and distinct significance. The meaning

THE LORD'S SUPPER

of this action, however, is the same, "The bread which I will give is my flesh, for the life of the world." (John 6 : 51.)

"*In like manner also the cup, after supper, saying, This cup is the new covenant in my blood: this do, as oft as ye drink it, in remembrance of me.*"

We have noted above, when describing the way to observe the Lord's Supper, how the Apostle omits here the mention of giving thanks over the cup, which is recorded by Matthew and Mark. We have since then remarked on the mistake made by many who sum up the meaning of the Lord's Supper in the name Eucharist. It is from this twice-repeated act of thanksgiving that they take encouragement in this notion. What may be made of it may be contemplated in the liturgy for the Eucharist contrived by those commonly known by the name of Irvingites, though an older and still more familiar example is to be found in the Romish Mass. Christ's giving thanks twice, in the usual manner of true piety when about to take food or dispense it to others, is no ground for contemplating the Lord's Supper as a rite expressive of solemn thanksgiving for the work of redemption. And had the Apostle Paul, like Matthew and Mark, made mention of the second act of thanksgiving, we would be right in refusing to take from that the suggestion that the Lord's Supper is to be observed as essentially a Eucharistic act of worship. Had Paul mentioned the second blessing, we would not be justified in omitting it when celebrating the Lord's Supper, even did we experience that its observance was attended with the danger of making the mistake referred to. We may be grateful, however, that the Apostle, by that authority he had from Christ, delivered the Lord's Supper to be observed without giving thanks over the cup. And having experience of the erroneous notions inferred from the double thanksgiving, and of their elaboration into a perversion of the simple meaning of the ordinance, we find an additional reason for what is the main contention of this tract, viz., the importance of a scrupulous adherence to the observance of the Lord's Supper in that form which has been prescribed in the Directory for Worship, which we contend is in accordance with the directory of the Apostle in 1 Cor. 11.

Taking the cup, that came on after supper in the Passover meal, Christ said, referring to the wine the cup contained, "*This cup is the new covenant in my blood.*" There is an obvious reference in these words, denoted by the word "new," to the old or Mosaic covenant; and the reference is equally plain to that solemn transaction by which that old covenant was published to Israel, and ratified by sacrifice and the sprinkling of blood. The people that were joined to God by that covenant, and the written instrument that embodied the covenant, and the tabernacle with all its furniture, that was to be the only place of worship, were all so sprinkled; by which sprinkling all were consecrated by blood to be what was required for the relations instituted by the old covenant. "And Moses took the blood, and sprinkled it on the people, and said, Behold the blood of the covenant which the LORD hath made with you." (Exod. 24 : 8.) In reference to this transaction, Christ said, "This is the new covenant in my blood." In this sense, as so used, "covenant" means "dispensation." Thus Christ announced to his Apostles what they were to publish to the world, viz., that the old dispensation was passed away, and he inaugurated a new one instead. It is again a covenant established in blood. But the blood is his own blood, which he "shed unto the remission of sins." The characteristic of the old covenant was the remembrance of sins, by repeated sacrifices and purifications with blood. The Lord Jesus brings in the new covenant prophesied by Jeremiah, the characteristic of which is, "their sins and their iniquities will I remember no more;" on which the inspired comment is, "Now where remission of these is, there is no more offering for sin." (Heb. 10:3, 17, 18.) Such is the covenant that is given to us in Christ's blood; for the covenant and the blood are the same, in the sense that an agreement and the bond that is the surety of the agreement are one.

Christ gave the cup to be drunk by the disciples, as he gave the bread to them to eat. All were to sup of that cup. "Drink ye all of it," is his recorded expression in Matthew. By this is denoted the common participation of all believers in the blood of Christ, with the benefit procured by it, which is the remission of sins, and reconciliation to God.

We may pause at this point to justify the objection made above to that interpretation of the meaning of the Lord's Supper that represents it as an observance wherein the believer binds himself by covenant to the Lord. It is from the word "covenant" in the words of the institution that this suggestion is taken. But here is no reference either to a covenant that Christ makes with his people, or to a covenant that the believer makes with Christ. It is a new dispensation that is published, and is called a covenant because enacted by God in the way of a covenant. It is the covenant of grace. It has been brought about and is now complete by reason of Christ's redeeming work. And so Christ says, "This *is* the new covenant." The dispensation has been inaugurated, and is established, and is here, no matter what men may do or not do. The cup is the sign of it; and as often as believers drink that cup, they exhibit that dispensation by showing the Lord's death, which is the surety of it. The operation of this covenant is the remission of sins, which is purely a dispensation of God, to be received by sinners through that grace that dispenses it, and by faith. All this is above men, and pertains purely to the sovereignty of God, and is of his covenanting, and not men's.

It is therefore no part of the meaning of the Lord's Supper that therein Christ is making a covenant with his disciples, or that he renews such a covenant as often as he meets them in this ordinance. Neither is it the meaning of the action of the communicant that he pledges himself to Christ in a covenant as between him and his Lord. There is, indeed, a covenant between Christ and the believers, as signified in Baptism; and the Lord's Supper is a suitable place to renew that covenant by a fresh act of spiritual consecration. But that is not the covenant signified by the cup. The covenant of the cup is as much the covenant it is when the cup is taken without faith, as when it is taken in faith; for the dispensation of the remission of sins is the present and abiding dispensation, and its benefit is offered to all, whether they will accept remission of sins through Christ or not. The worthy receiver, who by faith partakes of Christ's blood, receives the remission of his sins.

It is therefore expedient to keep apart these notions of the covenant in Christ's blood, and the believer's act of devoting himself to Christ in a spiritual manner. As an effective means to this, it is expedient to forbear using the word covenant for the latter, when at the Lord's table, seeing it tends to merging and confounding the two notions.

We have now to contemplate the action of the believer in this transaction. This action is an essential part of the ordinance, just as in any transaction the action of one party to it is as esssential as that of the other party. Viewing the ordinance as a language of signs, the action of the disciples is essential to the complete expression of that language, without which the language is mutilated, and no longer perfectly expresses what Christ appointed it to show forth. The Reformed churches, and particularly the Presbyterian churches that adhere to the Westminster Confession of Faith, properly insist, that in the Lord's Supper the communicants must not assume a passive posture, and suffer the bread to be put into their mouths by the ministrant. There must be action on their part. They must take their places as at a meal. They must receive the bread and wine by their own act, as those that need and take the food that is offered them. They must not receive alone, as if each ate for himself; but they eat in company, as recognizing one another in the transaction that signifies and seals their oneness of body and life, which is wrought in them by the body of Christ, and their common participation in the remission of sins, and in the dispensation of the new covenant. This is the Communion; and from this is derived one of the most appropriate names for the Lord's Supper. To this the Apostle gives emphatic expression in 1 Cor. 10:16: "The cup of blessing which we bless, is it not a communion of the blood of Christ? The bread [loaf] which we break, is it not a communion of the body of Christ?" The meaning of this communion is, not that there is any exchange between the disciples as communicating anything to one another; but a common participation of all the disciples in Christ. Not a mutual giving and taking between Christ and the disciples; but only Christ giving, and the disciples only receiving. The disciple being active and not merely passive, denotes that the reception of Christ and his benefits is voluntary, an action involving the assent of the mind and the co-operation of the will, and done intelligently, freely, and gladly.

The expressive signs of receiving and appropriating Christ's body and blood as he gives them are eating the bread and drinking the wine. These, and these only, are the signs appointed. In this the significance is complete. "The sacred character of the elements does not consist in themselves, but in their use. As soon as this use is completed, the bread and wine, whether in the body of the recipient or remaining in the vessels of the service, are no more holy than any other specimens of their kind in the world." (*Popular Lectures on Theological Themes*, A. A. Hodge, D.D., p. 40.)

Various customs have appeared in Christian Churches with regard to the bread and wine used in the Lord's Supper. Portions have been borne away from the table to be carried to the sick and others who in any way have been unable to be present at the communion, to be partaken of by such alone, as holy elements conveying special grace. In the Romish Mass care is taken to have no remnants whatever. The possible crumbs of the Host are wiped from the paten into the chalice, and the priest, drinking all the wine in the chalice, wipes it dry. The Book of Common Prayer of the Protestant Episcopal Church directs that "if any of the consecrated Bread and Wine remain after the Communion, it shall not be carried out of the Church; but the Minister and other Communicants shall, immediately after the Blessing, reverently eat and drink the same." All such treatment of the elements involves the notion of their having become something more than just bread and wine by reason of their relation to the Lord's Supper, and tends to fix attention on them, and to divert attention from the action and use connected with them, in which alone is to be found the true and simple, yet very impressive significance of the ordinance. As such they are therefore human additions, and so corruptions of the pure observance of the Lord's Supper.

Of these actions that constitute the whole transaction of the Lord's Supper, the Lord Jesus said, "*This do in remembrance of me.*" In the Apostle's directory, these words are said of the bread and the cup, each in its turn; and the meaning is especially emphasized by the Apostle's own affirmation, that concludes the directory, "For as often as ye eat this bread and drink this cup, ye proclaim the Lord's death till he come." These directions express very clearly what is the chief meaning of the Lord's Supper, and for what purpose it was instituted. It is to be a memorial celebration commemorating Christ—a commemoration that proclaims his death as the central fact of his personal appearance and work on earth, and as that which particularly makes him what he is to the believer and to the world, viz., the Saviour. It is a commemoration, as the Passover was. Instituting the Lord's Supper at that Passover meal, the injunction, "This do in remembrance of me," said each time, while appointing an eating and drinking for a custom, like that which they had been observing as the perpetuation of what was instituted by Moses along with the old covenant, and saying of the cup, "This is the new covenant," —in all this the Lord plainly intimated that he was giving a new commemoration that was to take the place of the old. His "This do in remembrance of me" meant, commemorate me and my death, as the departure out of Egypt has been commemorated. As that was the beginning of the old dispensation, so Christ's death is the beginning of the new dispensation. As the initial act of the old dispensation was commemorated till Christ came, so this commemoration of his death is to be perpetuated, and to proclaim his death till he comes again.

Thus this holy ordinance is a monument. As such it has its meaning, and accomplishes its purpose in a way quite distinct from the personal and private benefit attending it for those who celebrate it. This paramount meaning of the ordinance does not exclude the others that concern the communicants personally. On the contrary, it comprehends them as quite essential to that chief meaning and, to achieving that paramount purpose of proclaiming Christ's death till he come. For though a monument, it is a monument in action; not a pantomime, but really representing what it proclaims, by Christ's actually giving, and by the believers' actually "partaking of his body and blood to their spiritual nourishment and growth in grace." The monument stands in the action of true believers obeying Christ's ordinance as he gave it. The existence of true believers in perpetual succession is the condition of the perpetuation of the monument. With wonderful wisdom did Christ devise this monument. The very device is evidence of some identity of its Author with the Author of those only other monuments that bear comparison with this one—we mean the Sabbath day and the Passover.

"The master said when he instituted it, 'This do in remembrance of me.' And ever since that awful night, endless successions of disciples have gathered to perform these sacred rites, with the intention of 'showing forth his death till he come.'

"The great mass of men pass away in indistinguishable throngs, falling like leaves of the forest in mass, their individuality lost to human recollection in this world forever. The memories of some few men out of the thousands linger long and fade slowly into the night of oblivion. A very few epoch-making men, as Moses, Paul, Augustine, Luther, change the course of human history and live forever in the new world they inaugurate. But it is only Christ the incarnate God, Christ the perfect man, Christ the bleeding Price of man's redemption, Christ the resurgent Victor over death and hell, whose ever-present memory is the condition of all progressive thought and life. The memory of Christ as the great character of all history has become omnipresent in all literature, philosophy, ethics, politics, and life. All experience, all existence, witness to him. The whole universe repeats his story and keeps him eternally in mind. Monuments (*monere*) exist to keep persons and events in mind. They are of many kinds, as of earth, or stone, or brass, or changes wrought in the forms of human speech or action, or other observances to be repeated forever at intervals. This latter kind are incomparably more effective and imperishable as memorials than the others. The Tower of Babel, the Pyramids of Egypt, the most stupendous monuments the world has ever seen, have either perished or are far gone in decay, while the history they were erected to commemorate is lost beyond the rational guess of critics. And yet the Sabbath-day monument of creation, thousands of years older than the Pyramids, and the Lord's Supper, which in its historic roots in the Passover was brought into being at the very feet of the then young Pyramids themselves, remain as fresh and as articulate with their original significance as at their birth. These observational monuments are likewise omnipresent the world over, as well as imperishable. The Lord's Day and the Lord's Supper, preserved and disseminated with absolutely unbroken continuity down the ages and throughout the nations, keep the memory of Christ alive just as it was at first, because their very existence and constant repetition are the unfaded testimony of Christ's contemporaries, the accumulated testimony of all ages, that Jesus Christ was in very fact delivered sacrificially for our offences, and raised again for our justification. (Rom. 4 : 25.)"—*Popular Lectures on Theological Themes, Dr. A. A. Hodge,* pp. 403, 404.

Our subject has now been treated with sufficient completeness to permit us to lay it down. We have tried to present it in a way to make it profitable, even apart from the present contest about the wine of the Communion, and also other controversial matters involved in it. Controversy, however, has ever attended the subject of the Lord's Supper from the beginning; and Christians must expect that it always will. This is inevitable, from the very nature of the ordinance. It was instituted to proclaim the death of Christ till he came again. It is the standard of the Church militant; and those who maintain it in its integrity are the true standard bearers. What is so central in the Church as organized, and so identified with the true doctrine of Christ and the life of believers, is sure to feel, and feel quickly, all the hurtful and corrupting influences that invade the Church and turn believers from the faith. The standard bearer in battle is sure to be in the thickest of the fight. Therefore, like the boon of civil liberty, the Lord's Supper and its benefits are only to be preserved at the cost of perpetual vigilance. When believers resign themselves to the thought that controversy is past, and that this ordinance may be enjoyed without the need of watchfulness against invasion, surrender of some sort is sure to follow. The survey of our subject illustrates this. It shows, also, that surrender at one point, the admission of *any* change in what was instituted to be perpetuated unchanged, concedes the right to make other changes, and reflects on the wisdom of those who renounced the changes of the past and restored the ordinance to that pure observance of it that they handed down to us. Let the reader, who is not otherwise familiar with the facts, contemplate the actual invasions of the simple observance of the Lord's Supper that have taken place, as noted in this tract. Let him add to these as many more that have not been noted. Let him remember that whatever omission, change, or addition has been proposed, has had, in the minds of the proposers, as much justification as the proposed rejection of the wine of the Communion;

and let him reflect that this generation has no right to make its change, without accepting the changes of those who have gone before, and conceding those that may be urged hereafter. Then what becomes of this precious ordinance? Did we now have a form of observing the Lord's Supper that embodied only all the changes passionately urged in the past, it would be something so totally unlike what was originally instituted as to be unrecognizable as the same thing. Such a situation could only betoken a total departure from true Christianity. The case is not imaginary. It is actually realized in some parts of the nominal Church. Not, indeed, that anywhere all the changes ever attempted are to be found embodied in one form of observance. But in some places there are so many changes, and these combined with so much superstition, or mere formality and display, as utterly to degrade the ordinance and make it the exponent of spiritual death, if not of heathenism itself.

That we are privileged to enjoy the ordinance in its purity, is due to the fidelity of those who were before us. We shall prove ourselves to be their unworthy successors if we do not preserve and transmit in its purity what they recovered and transmitted to us.

COMMUNION WINE

By the Rev. Dunlop Moore, D.D., New Brighton, Pa.

In discussing briefly the question whether the wine proper to be employed in the observance of the Lord's Supper is the fermented or the unfermented juice of the grape, we remark:

1. This is a modern question. It is only of late years that the opinion has been expressed that Christ's command to drink the cup of the Eucharist referred to an unfermented liquid. We have never seen a genuine quotation from a Christian author, who wrote before the present century, in which it was asserted, or even hinted, that "the fruit of the vine" with which our Saviour instituted the Communion, was the unfermented juice of the grape. It can be demonstrated that the Westminster divines, who have taught in the Shorter Catechism that the Lord's Supper is to be celebrated "by giving and receiving bread and wine," took the word "wine" in its proper and usual meaning, and had no idea of what is now called "unfermented wine." The employment of "unfermented wine" in the Sacrament of the Supper is an innovation of the nineteenth century, and a departure from the practice of the Church Universal in all previous ages.

2. The Bible nowhere divides wine into fermented and unfermented, lawful and unlawful. Distilled spirits do not appear to have been known of old among the Israelites. But any fermented drink known to them they were allowed by the law to partake of. (Deut. 14:26.) The first mention in Scripture of wine (*yayin*) exhibits it as a drink that, taken in excess, causes intoxication. (Gen. 9:20, 21). Hence, when the next mention of wine (*yayin*) occurs in Scripture without any indication of distinction, we are compelled to understand by "wine" the same natural product whose intoxicating property had been already signified. But when Moses next makes mention of wine, it appears as a lawful refreshment. (Gen. 14:18.) The sacred volume, after first letting us know the inebriating quality of what is called wine, proceeds to speak of wine without distinguishing it into different kinds, and lets us see it now causing mischief, now used lawfully. It would be to imitate conjurors, who draw from the same opening in a vessel wine and water, if we should make the same unqualified word wine (*yayin*), as used in the same narrative, yield two liquors possessed of essentially different qualities. Moreover, so rigorous an observer of the law of God as Nehemiah had "all sorts of wine" occasionally on his table. (Neh. 5:18.) He was the cupbearer of the king of Persia, and we know that the wine which he was accustomed to handle could intoxicate. (Esther 1:10.) The same wine is, in Prov. 31:4-6, disallowed to some and prescribed to others. The wine which was given by Abigail to David for refreshment appears as belonging to the same store on which her husband Nabal got drunk. (1 Sam. 25:18, 36.) That *all* wine kept by the Jews in bottles or jars was intoxicating is clear from Jer. 13:12, 13. *Every* bottle filled with wine could cause drunkenness. No moralist — Jewish, Christian, or heathen —

has ever, in condemning wine or advocating temperance, alluded to the existence of a wine which might be drunk without risk. This fact, if duly weighed, must lead to the rejection of the so-called "two-wine theory" which is now advocated by some in the interest of temperance. It has no foundation in Hebrew or classical antiquity. It has been always customary to hold that the same wine (like the same money or the same tongue) could be a blessing or a curse according to the use made of it. In illustration of this point, it is enough to refer here to Jesus the son of Sirach in *Ecclesiasticus* 31 : 25–30 ; Socrates in the *Symposium* of Xenphon. close of second part; Pliny, *Natural History*, 14 : 7 ; Clement of Alexandria, *Pædagogus*, chap. 2, " On Drinking." As Dr. W. H. Green, of Princeton, has emphatically affirmed : When wine, either in the Bible or out of it, " is approved or disapproved, this is not due to the different character of the wine itself, but to its rational or immoderate use."

3. That the wine approved of in the New Testament could intoxicate must be evident to every one who studies John 2 : 10, or who compares 1 Tim. 5 : 23 with Eph. 5 : 18. Timothy, who was living in Ephesus (1 Tim. 1 : 3), was directed to use for his stomach's sake and often infirmities "a little" of the wine (*oinos*) on which the Ephesians were forbidden to be drunk. If there were no danger, too, in the use of this good wholesome wine, why should only a little of it be prescribed? Deacons (1 Tim. 3 : 8) and aged women (Tit. 2 : 3) must not be addicted to " much wine." The injunction of moderation in these cases proves that the good wine, whose use is sanctioned, could not be unfermented, unintoxicating grape juice. There is a temptation in the use of that wine which " makes glad the heart of man " (Ps. 104 : 15), or exhilarates, to drink it too freely, and so to become intoxicated by it. Which effect, exhilaration or intoxication, shall be produced by wine, depends on the quantity drunk, just as whether a man shall be invigorated or tired out by walking, depends on the amount of exercise he takes.

4. There is now no unfermented wine in use among the natives of Syria and Palestine. Dr. Selah Merrill, U. S. consul in Jerusalem, and archæologist of the American Palestine Exploration Society, who tells us that he observed this matter closely, writes in contradiction of the statement that Palestinean wine would not intoxicate : " The fact is, the use of the wine of Palestine produces the legitimate and natural effects of wine ; that is, it exhilarates and intoxicates." Dr. W. M. Thomson, author of *The Land and the Book*, in the third volume, p. 236, tells us : " Wine is the fermented juice of the grape . . . No other kind of wine is known in Syria, and, so far as can be ascertained, it never had any actual existence. There is no evidence that there has occurred any important variation in the manufacture, the use, or the effects of wine from remote antiquity." The day when ignorance regarding the real character of the wines of Syria and Palestine was excusable, is now past. Sometimes *dibs* is represented as an unfermented wine of Palestine. But it is simply honey of grapes, and is not drunk, but used as a preserve. To call *dibs*, wine, as some advocates of temperance have done, is, in the language of Prof. E. Post, M.D., Beirut, Syria, a most competent witness, "to trifle with the text and meaning of Scripture." Dr. A. A. Hodge was fully justified in declaring that "the traditions of the Fathers, the consensus of the churches, the history of the past, the scholarship of the present, the testimony of travelers and missionaries stand as one unbroken wall in testimony to the fact that to become WINE it is necessary that the juice of the grape should be fermented. This is so true that any real or apparent testimony to the contrary is received only as a puzzle of eccentricity or of accident."

5. In support of the two-wine hypothesis, the chief linguistic argument relied on is the occurrence of such expressions in Scripture as the *treading out of wine* (Isa. 16 : 10) and the *gathering of wine* (Jer. 40 : 10). Hence it is said fresh grape juice is a proper meaning of wine (*yayin*). But in Psalm 104 : 14, bread (see Hebrew text) is described as "brought forth out of the earth." Is, therefore, grain, bread? Again, we read in Job 28 : 2, "Iron is taken out of the earth." Is, therefore, unsmelted ore, proper iron? What sorry work might be made with Scripture by refusing to allow the use of the figure prolepsis in such examples! We read in our English Bible that Abraham commanded Eliezer to "take a wife" for his son. (Gen. 24 : 7.) He brought a virgin (v. 43) in the execution of this commission. We ask: Was Eliezer instructed to choose a married woman, a wife, to be the spouse of Isaac? and is "virgin" one of the proper meanings of "wife"? If it be said that in the charge of Abraham there is a prolepsis, and that his servant was instructed to take for Isaac one who should become a wife to him, then, on the same principle, we can vindicate everywhere in Scripture to the word *yayin*, or wine, the meaning in which it is first introduced to us, namely, the fermented juice of the grape. When "wife" means a virgin in Scripture, when "iron" means unsmelted ore, and "bread" simple unground grain, then wine can, by the same process of interpretation, mean the fresh juice of the grape. As to the passage in Gen. 40 : 11, we would remark that with the same facility with which the practice of drinking in Egypt fresh grape juice is proved from it, we could prove from the context that in that country it was customary of old for lean kine to eat up fat kine, and for thin ears of corn to swallow up good ears. The symbolical representations of a dream or of sculpture cannot be read as plain prose.

The wine with which God blessed Israel is described in Deut. 32 : 14: "Thou didst drink the pure blood of the grape." In the Revised Version the rendering runs: "And of the blood of the grape thou drankest wine." The word here rendered "wine" is *chemer*. Gesenius, Keil, J. A. Alexander, and all critical commentaries make this word to denote etymologically a fermented drink. And missionaries who use the Arabic and Syriac languages assure us that by the Arabic and Syriac forms of the word—*chamr* and *chamro*—nothing but a fermented drink can be denoted. Every one acquainted with Hebrew sees that this passage, which is so often quoted as testifying in favor of an unfermented wine, testifies, on the contrary, that the wine with which God blessed his people was certainly fermented. The very name here given to it makes this point evident to the Shemitic scholar. We do not believe that there is now in America a Hebrew professor of reputation who would deny that the good, approved wine of the Bible is the fermented juice of the grape.

6. Our Lord, in instituting the holy Supper, called the contents of the cup, "the fruit of the vine." Why did he use this expression? Simply because the Jews of his day employed the phrase to designate the wine partaken of on sacred occasions, as at the Passover and on the evening of the Sabbath. Our Lord did not invent the expression, but availed himself of it in instituting the Supper after the Passover, because it, and no other expression, was employed to denote wine by his countrymen at that festival. The Mishna, "On Blessings," expressly states that in blessing wine, or *yayin*, it is to be called "the fruit of the vine." The fruit of the vine is strictly the grape; but we must have respect to Jewish usage in interpreting the phrase. We avail ourselves of our knowledge of Jewish usage of language in making the Evangelists declare that our Lord rose from the dead

on the first day of the week. Without consulting rabbinical usage, we could not tell that *mia tōn Sabbatōn* meant the first day of the week. From the same rabbinical usage we can ascertain that in the time of Christ (as now) "the fruit of the vine" was a phrase that denoted neither fresh grape juice (*tirosh* or *asis*) nor vinegar, but real wine, *yayin*. How natural is this designation of wine is seen from Herodotus, book i. 212, where the wine by which the Massagetae were overcome is called "the fruit of the vine"! "The fruit of the vine" is employed by no author as a term to designate "unintoxicating wine." By consulting 1 Cor. 11 : 21 we learn that, in celebrating the Lord's Supper in the Church at Corinth, some of the communicants were "drunken." These unworthy members could get drunk on "the fruit of the vine." This testimony of Scripture is decisive as to what "the fruit of the vine" denotes. We add that bread and wine (*yayin* or *oinos*) are invariably associated in the Bible. Never is bread associated with new wine. When, then, one element of the Supper is bread, the other element, according to Scriptural usage, is not fresh grape juice, but real wine. If unground grain were eaten at the Supper, then *tirosh*, or must, would, according to Scripture, be its appropriate accompaniment. There is, too, no evidence that the Jews ever tried to keep must from fermentation. Thus every consideration shows that real wine, the fermented juice of the grape, is the proper element in the Supper of the Lord.

7. When people say that no fermented wine could be used in the Passover, they only display their ignorance of Jewish customs. No passage from the Talmud or authoritative work on Jewish usages has ever been quoted in which the use of the pure fermented juice of the grape is forbidden at the Passover. There are statements in the Talmud which show that the wine used in the Passover must have been intoxicating. Provision is made to prevent it from producing drunkenness. Drinks made of five specified kinds of *grain* are forbidden during the Passover. But drinks of the fermented juice of grapes and other *fruits*, when carefully prepared by Israelites, are lawful. It is amazing what false statements regarding the wine of the Passover are put forward by those who ought to have taken greater care to ascertain the truth. Jewish Rabbis are represented as affirming what they did not say. Thus, in Dr. A. J. Gordon's tract, *Fermented Wine; or, The Fruit of the Vine*, the Rev. S. Morais, of Philadelphia, is made to say that it is contrary to the law of Moses and all the traditions of the Jews to use fermented wine at the Passover. But this Rabbi, in a letter published in the *Christian Quarterly Review* for July, 1886, states: "The nature of the fermentation prohibited to Israelites on Passover is exclusively that which belongs to grain products. Wines were always, and are now, drunk on that holiday by men considered rigid adherents of the law. It is impossible that any Rabbi, or any Hebrew acquainted with his religion, should have contradicted this fact." Dr. Delitzsch, who knew well what he said, writes in the *Expositor*, January, 1886: "The Jewish Passover wine is really fermented, and only as a substitute in case of need, is unfermented wine permitted. Thus it was fermented wine, too, which Jesus handed to the disciples at his parting meal." Never do the Scriptures speak of a leavened *liquor*. Christ drank vinegar (which is fermented) during the Passover. (John 19 : 30.)

But it may be said: In employing unfermented grape juice in the Supper we are using "the fruit of the vine," and so fulfilling the commandment to drink of the cup. In the same way, one might pretend to fulfill the commandment to love his neighbor by loving the person living in the next house. The question for us is, What did our Lord mean, in enjoining on us to drink "the fruit of the vine"? The worst of all deceptions is that of keeping the word of promise to the ear, and breaking it to the heart. We dare not warp our Lord's words from their real intent by alleging that according to their letter they might mean something which was certainly not in his mind in using them. And in our zeal for the promotion of temperance we must beware of making any change in the Supper of the Lord, which would involve a reflexion on the wisdom or holiness of him who instituted that ordinance.

8. The wine of the Communion certainly did not differ from the wine used in the drink offering under the law. Now let this point be well marked. What the Israelites were required in tithing to consecrate to the Lord is called *tirosh*, or new wine; what was actually presented in the drink offering is called *yayin*, or wine. If unfermented grape juice was used in the drink offering, why is neither of the two words, that properly denote this liquid, ever employed in connection with the drink offering? Why is the word *yayin* used, whose quality we know from its effect on Noah, Lot, and others, and in regard to an unintoxicating kind of which Scripture is absolutely silent? Indeed, the very wine of the drink offering is once called *strong drink*. (Num. 28:7, Rev. Vers.) In the Mishna, in the treatise on "Tithes," we are told that wine was tithed when it was in the course of fermentation. No effort could have been made to keep it from completing the process; for in the Mishna, *Menachoth* 8:6, wine, *sweet*, or *fumigated*, or *boiled*, is pronounced unfit for offerings. What we know of the wine of the drink offering lets us perceive the significance of the prohibition given to the priests, "Do not drink wine nor strong drink . . . *when ye go into the tabernacle*." (Lev. 10:9.) What kind of wine was it which priests could drink in *the inner court* of the sanctuary? (Ezek. 44:21.) What, too, was the wine offered to the Rechabites in *one of the chambers of the house of the Lord?* (Jer. 35:2.) Was it not wine which could intoxicate? Was it not such wine as was used in the drink offering? The Targum of Jonathan will not allow wine of less than forty days old to be poured out before the Lord. (On Num. 28:7.) This time was judged requisite for the fresh juice of the grape to attain by fermenting the quality of wine.

9. In regard to the alleged danger of using real wine in the Communion, we will allow Dr. Willis J. Beecher to speak: " Nor does any great weight seem properly to attach to the argument commonly cited against the use of fermented wines at the Lord's table, namely, that the dormant appetites of inebriates are thereby reawakened, so that many are led to relapse into drunken habits. One should not be accused of unreasonable incredulity, if he is pretty sceptical in regard to alleged instances of this sort. A person at the Communion table is so situated that he cannot immediately indulge the reawakened appetite, even if appetite should be reawakened. He is restrained from yielding to the temptation thus presented until he has first had time for reflection. He is surrounded by specially strong influences to help him to conquer temptation."

We are safe in observing in the proper frame of mind whatsoever the Lord has commanded us to do at his table.

" Morality may spare
Her grave concern, her kind suspicion there."

Those who desire to read a fuller discussion of this subject, can consult the articles on " The Bible Wine Question " and on " Sacramental Wine," in the *Presbyterian Review* for January, 1881, and January, 1882.

www.ingramcontent.com/pod-product-compliance
Lightning Source LLC
Chambersburg PA
CBHW020142170426
43199CB00010B/856